U.S. American Politics
Reader

Mark R. Joslyn
University of Kansas

Kendall Hunt
publishing company

Cover image © used under license from Shutterstock, Inc.

Kendall Hunt
publishing company

www.kendallhunt.com
Send all inquiries to:
4050 Westmark Drive
Dubuque, IA 52004-1840

Printed in the United States of America
10 9 8 7 6 5 4 3 2

CONTENTS

iv   Contents

PART I

American Political Culture

CHAPTER 1

Individualism

Habits of the Heart:
Individualism and Commitment in American Life

Robert Bellah

In *Habits of the Heart,* Bellah, et al., introduce individualism, a key component of American political culture. The authors also address important themes in political culture such as community and public and private life. Pay close attention to the linkages between these topics and their potential effects on political affairs.

Individualism lies at the very core of American culture. Every one of the four traditions we have singled out is in a profound sense individualistic. There is a biblical individualism and a civic individualism as well as a utilitarian and an expressive individualism. Whatever the differences among the traditions and the consequent differences in their understandings of individualism, there are some things they all share, things that are basic to American identity. We believe in the dignity, indeed the sacredness, of the individual. Anything that would violate our right to think for ourselves, judge for ourselves, make our own decisions, live our lives as we see fit, is not only morally wrong, it is sacrilegious. Our highest and noblest aspirations, not only for ourselves, but for those we care about, for our society and for the

world, are closely linked to our individualism. But individualism has come to mean so many things and to contain such contradictions and paradoxes that even to defend it requires that we analyze it critically, that we consider especially those tendencies that would destroy it from within.

A deep and continuing theme in American literature is the hero who must leave society, alone or with one or a few others, in order to realize the moral good in the wilderness, at sea, or on the margins of settled society. Sometimes the withdrawal involves a contribution to society, as in James Fenimore Cooper's *The Deerslayer.* Sometimes the new marginal community realizes ethical ends impossible in the larger society, as in the interracial harmony between Huckleberry

Finn and Jim. Sometimes the flight from society is simply mad and ends in general disaster, as in *Moby Dick*. When it is not in and through society but in flight from it that the good is to be realized, as in the case of Melville's Ahab, the line between ethical heroism and madness vanishes, and the destructive potentiality of a completely asocial individualism is revealed.

America is also the inventor of that most mythic individual hero, the cowboy, who again and again saves a society he can never completely fit into. The cowboy has a special talent—he can shoot straighter and faster than other men—and a special sense of justice. But these characteristics make him so unique that he can never fully belong to society. His destiny is to defend society without ever really joining it. He rides off alone into the sunset like Shane, or like the Lone Ranger moves on accompanied only by his Indian companion. But the cowboy's importance is not that he is isolated or antisocial. Rather, his significance lies in his unique, individual virtue and special skill and it is because of those qualities that society needs and welcomes him. Shane, after all, starts as a real outsider, but ends up with the gratitude of the community and the love of a woman and a boy. And while the Lone Ranger never settles down and marries the local schoolteacher, he always leaves with the affection and gratitude of the people he has helped. It is as if the myth says you can be a truly good person, worthy of admiration and love, only if you resist fully joining the group. But sometimes the tension leads to an irreparable break. Will Kane, the hero of *High Noon*, abandoned by the cowardly townspeople, saves them from an unrestrained killer, but then throws his sheriff's badge in the dust and goes off into the desert with his bride. One is left wondering where they will go, for there is no longer any link with any town.

The connection of moral courage and lonely individualism is even tighter for that other, more modern American hero, the hard-boiled detective. From Sam Spade to Serpico, the detective is a loner. He is often unsuccessful in conventional terms, working out of a shabby office where the phone never rings. Wily, tough, smart, he is

nonetheless unappreciated. But his marginality is also his strength. When a bit of business finally comes their way, Philip Marlowe, Lew Archer, and Travis McGee are tenacious. They pursue justice and help the unprotected even when it threatens to unravel the fabric of society itself. Indeed, what is remarkable about the American detective story is less its hero than its image of crime. When the detective begins his quest, it appears to be an isolated incident. But as it develops, the case turns out to be linked to the powerful and privileged of the community. Society, particularly "high society," is corrupt to the core. It is this boring into the center of society to find it rotten that constitutes the fundamental drama of the American detective story. It is not a personal but a social mystery that the detective must unravel.

To seek justice in a corrupt society, the American detective must be tough, and above all, he must be a loner. He lives outside the normal bourgeois pattern of career and family. As his investigations begin to lead him beyond the initial crime to the glamorous and powerful center of the society, its leaders make attempts to buy off the detective, to corrupt him with money, power, or sex. This counterpoint to the gradual unravelling of the crime is the battle the detective wages for his own integrity, in the end rejecting the money of the powerful and spurning (sometimes jailing or killing) the beautiful woman who has tried to seduce him. The hard-boiled detective, who may long for love and success, for a place in society, is finally driven to stand alone, resisting the blandishments of society, to pursue a lonely crusade for justice. Sometimes, as in the film *Chinatown*, corruption is so powerful and so total that the honest detective no longer has a place to stand and the message is one of unrelieved cynicism.

Both the cowboy and the hard-boiled detective tell us something important about American individualism. The cowboy, like the detective, can be valuable to society only because he is a completely autonomous individual who stands outside it. To serve society, one must be able to stand alone, not needing others, not depending on their judgment, and not submitting to their wishes. Yet this individualism is not selfishness. Indeed, it is a kind of heroic selflessness. One accepts the necessity of remaining alone in order to serve the values of the group. And this obligation to aloneness is an important key to the American moral imagination. Yet it is part of the profound ambiguity of the mythology of American individualism that its moral heroism is always just a step away from despair. For an Ahab, and occasionally for a cowboy or a detective, there is no return to society, no moral redemption.

It is now time to consider what a self that is not empty would be like—one that is constituted rather than unencumbered, one that has, let us admit it, encumbrances, but whose encumbrances make connection to others easier and more natural. Just as the empty self makes sense in a particular institutional context—that of the upward mobility of the middle-class individual who must leave home and church in order to succeed in an impersonal world of rationality and competition— so a constituted self makes sense in terms of another institutional context, what we would call, in the full sense of the word, community.

Communities, in the sense in which we are using the term, have a history—in an important sense they are constituted by their past—and for this reason we can speak of a real community as a "community of memory," one that does not forget its past. In order not to forget that past, a community is involved in retelling its story, its constitutive narrative, and in so doing, it offers examples of the men and women who have embodied and exemplified the meaning of the community. These stories of collective history and exemplary individuals are an important part of the tradition that is so central to a community of memory.

Examples of such genuine communities are not hard to find in the United States. There are ethnic and racial communities, each with its own story and its own heroes and heroines. There are religious communities that recall and reenact their stories in the weekly and annual cycles of their ritual year, remembering the scriptural stories that tell them who they are and the saints and

martyrs who define their identity. There is the national community, defined by its history and by the character of its representative leaders from John Winthrop to Martin Luther King, Jr. Americans identify with their national community partly because there is little else that we all share in common but also partly because America's history exemplifies aspirations widely shared throughout the world: the ideal of a free society, respecting all its citizens, however diverse, and allowing them all to fulfill themselves. Yet some Americans also remember the history of suffering inflicted and the gap between promise and realization, which has always been very great. At some times, neighborhoods, localities, and regions have been communities in America, but that has been hard to sustain in our restless and mobile society. Families can be communities, remembering their past, telling the children the stories of parents' and grandparents' lives, and sustaining hope for the future—though without the context of a larger community that sense of family is hard to maintain. Where history and hope are forgotten and community means only the gathering of the similar, community degenerates into lifestyle enclave. The temptation toward that transformation is endemic in America, though the transition is seldom complete.

People growing up in communities of memory not only hear the stories that tell how the community came to be, what its hopes and fears are, and how its ideals are exemplified in outstanding men and women; they also participate in the practices— ritual, aesthetic, ethical—that define the community as a way of life. We call these "practices of commitment" for they define the patterns of loyalty and obligation that keep the community alive. And if the language of the self-reliant individual is the first language of American moral life, the languages of tradition and commitment in communities of memory are "second languages" that most Americans know as well, and which they use when the language of the radically separate self does not seem adequate.

Sometimes Americans make a rather sharp dichotomy between private and public life. Viewing one's primary task as "finding oneself" in autonomous self-reliance, separating oneself not only from one's parents but also from those larger communities and traditions that constitute one's past, leads to the notion that it is in oneself, perhaps in relation to a few intimate others, that fulfillment is to be found. Individualism of this sort often implies a negative view of public life. The impersonal forces of the economic and political worlds are what the individual needs protection against. In this perspective, even occupation, which has been so central to the identity of Americans in the past, becomes instrumental—not a good in itself, but only a means to the attainment of a rich and satisfying private life. But on the basis of what we have seen in our observation of middle-class American life, it would seem that this quest for purely private fulfillment is illusory: it often ends in emptiness instead. On the other hand, we found many people, some of whom we introduced earlier in this chapter, for whom private fulfillment and public involvement are not antithetical. These people evince an individualism that is not empty but is full of content drawn from an active identification with communities and traditions. Perhaps the notion that private life and public life are at odds is incorrect. Perhaps they are so deeply involved with each other that the impoverishment of one entails the

impoverishment of the other. Parker Palmer is probably right when he says that "in a healthy society the private and the public are not mutually exclusive, not in competition with each other. They are, instead, two halves of a whole, two poles of a paradox. They work together dialectically, helping to create and nurture one another."

Certainly this dialectical relationship is clear where public life degenerates into violence and fear. One cannot live a rich private life in a state of siege, mistrusting all strangers and turning one's home into an armed camp. A minimum of public decency and civility is a precondition for a fulfilling private life. On the other hand, public involvement is often difficult and demanding. To engage successfully in the public world, one needs personal strength and the support of family and friends. A rewarding private life is one of the preconditions for a healthy public life.

For all their doubts about the public sphere, Americans are more engaged in voluntary associations and civic organizations than the citizens of most other industrial nations. In spite of all the difficulties, many Americans feel they must "get involved." In public life as in private, we can discern the habits of the heart that sustain individualism and commitment, as well as what makes them problematic.

Chapter 1 Exercise

Define individualism. Why is individualism important to understanding American Political Culture?

Is there a connection between government and individualism?

PART II

Constructing the Constitution

CHAPTER 2

Compromises

"To Form a More Perfect Union . . ."

Robin U. Russin

In *To Form a More Perfect Union*, Robin Russin describes the political environment that preceded the writing of our Constitution and the political compromises sought at the constitutional convention. He emphasizes the strong personalities and political ambitions of the founders, noting the importance of personal characteristics in determining the successes and failures in Philadelphia. In the end, our Constitution did not "come down to us from the mountain like the tablets of Moses." Rather, it is a "Human Document," the product of political compromise and human imperfection.

The creation of the Constitution was nothing less than the second American revolution.

Less than ten years after the signing of the Declaration of Independence, the loose confederation of ex-colonies that formed the United States was in chaos, threatened by internal strife and foreign intrigue. In the wake of the Revolution Washington had marveled, "Who, that was not a witness, could imagine that the most violent local prejudices would cease so soon; and that men who came from different parts of the continent, strongly disposed by the habits of education to despise and quarrel with one another, would

instantly become but one band of brothers?" And yet, with the shots of Lexington and Concord still ringing in their ears, but without an enemy presence or a sense of common purpose to bind them, the men who had spoken and fought so bravely for the cause of liberty in the New World were now in danger of losing everything.

The Revolution had in fact been a civil war and had left deep and bitter divisions in the country, a legacy of bad blood and distrust. In government there was no president, no Supreme Court, only a Congress so weak that most of its members never bothered to attend. The country was hopelessly in debt, unable to pay even the interest on its loans, with the original Articles of

---

"To Form a More Perfect Union . . . ," and "A Constitutional Add-On: Ten Amendments to Protect the Individual Rights of Citizens," by Robin U. Russin as appeared in *Harvard Magazine*, May/June 1987. Reprinted by permission of the author.

Confederation allowing no national powers of trade regulation, taxation, or even effective military defense. Drastic action was needed and yet none seemed possible. The new experiment in freedom drifted ever closer to destruction.

In retrospect we have come to take the Constitution for granted as a natural outcome of the Revolution. It hardly seems possible that it was the product of debate and compromise—struggled over, endlessly revised and rewritten—and not gifted to us as an eternal mandate from some higher power. The Constitutional Convention is known to most Americans, if at all, as hardly more than a procedural formality, a footnote in our history. In truth it was a daring and uncertain venture, in fact almost treasonous, since its implied purpose was the overthrow of the existing government. Perhaps that is why the Constitution has endured so well; the tensions it addresses and embodies are largely still with us—the challenges to human rights, the financial struggles of farmers and tradesmen, the difficulty of giving each and every person his or her "inalienable" chance to live and prosper as an "equal" citizen under the law. As we approach the Constitution's bicentennial birthday, it is hard to imagine how new, how visionary was that agenda two hundred years ago.

The new nation's problems were legion. For one thing, the states were far from united; each viewed itself as a sovereign power, with disastrous consequences. Between them, jealousies and economic battles arose. States such as New York and Rhode Island were actually drifting toward a secessionist stance, hoping to go it alone. Traders who wanted to engage in interstate commerce often had to pay two tariffs, one going and one returning, stifling an already ruinous economy. Northerners were embarrassed by the presence of slavery in the South; Southern states, their economies dependent on "the Africans," resented any interference. Travel and communications were difficult—news of the Declaration had crossed the Atlantic almost before it had crossed the Alleghenies. The Carolinas and Georgia were so different from even the middle states that to some they seemed like strange tropical fiefdoms, more West Indian than "American." And states were often torn by internal strife, as the Tennessee area sought to split away from North Carolina, Kentucky from Virginia, and New York and New Hampshire wrestled over what is now Vermont. There was no central authority to adjudicate what course expansion into the West would take.

The financial situation was a nightmare. Without a common currency or set of standards, merchants tore their hair over interstate exchange: French sovereigns and Spanish pieces of eight were traded alongside doubloons, British sterling, gold johannes, moidores, pistoles, and hundreds of independent state mintings, creating chaos in the marketplace. Pieces of eight and dollars were worth six shillings in New England, eight in New York, seven in Pennsylvania, and 32 in South Carolina. Good hard currency was in short supply, and coins were commonly "shaved" to stretch their value, the shavings melted down for the precious metals. Forgery was such a problem that when Rufus King, of the Massachusetts legislature, received a shipment of supposedly safe, newly minted money, all of it was counterfeit.

To make things worse, a number of states without sufficient hard assets were independently experimenting with paper money, in a situation that prefigured events in Weimar Germany, the market was flooded with paper in the hope of paying off debt, making farmers and manufacturers afraid to sell their products in return for currency that was devalued daily. The old Continental dollar bills were so useless that one satirical fellow used them to wallpaper his barbershop; in Philadelphia, a mob of men and boys festooned their hats with money one day and paraded an unhappy mutt they had tarred and feathered in worthless bills.

Common citizens especially found themselves longing for the good old days of British stability. Farm foreclosures became commonplace, and class tensions ran high. The jails were overflowing with debtors and the dispossessed, and conditions were terrible; one prisoner described himself as "alive, and that is all, as I am full of boils and putrefied sores all over my body and they make me stink alive, besides having some of my feet froze." In Massachusetts, Shays's Rebellion, an uprising of desperate farmers, threatened to bring down the state government. The farmers surrounded courthouses from Northampton to Worcester in order to dramatize the poverty that worthless money and legal manipulation had inflicted on them, green sprigs in their hatbands to symbolize "natural" law. For these people, democracy had failed.

The Revolutionary veterans themselves, unpaid and restive, posed a grave threat. In 1783 inflammatory, "anonymous" pamphlets, circulated by those discontented with the current leadership, urged the army to throw down the new government. "Imagine," wrote Finance Minister Robert Morris, "an army ready to disband or mutiny," threatening "a government whose sole authority consists in the power of framing recommendations." In one of the great dramatic moments in our history, Washington called for a meeting of the army and spoke to the hostile crowd. "Gentlemen, you will permit me to put on my spectacles," he said, "for I have grown not only gray, but almost blind, in the service of my country." As had happened before and would again, Washington turned the tide, leaving the assembly in tears when he begged them not to "deluge our rising empire in blood." Even so, a band of eighty troops from Pennsylvania marched on Philadelphia and humiliated the Congress, which could do nothing to stop the harassment.

The bold men who had faced and beaten the British empire were paralyzed by their distrust of a strong central government.

Europe was only too happy to contribute to the confusion. In vain did John Adams attempt to enforce the Treaty of Peace worked out at the end of the Revolution. Britain, still America's chief trading partner, insisted on allowing only business using British ships and actually kept illegal military posts along the major American waterways to enforce its monopoly, citing America's inability to pay off the war debt and refusal to return confiscated Tory property as its excuse. Largely dependent on the shipping trade, the hard-hit northern states attempted an embargo against England, only to find the middle and southern states stabbing them in the back by declaring free ports for trade with the British. Those American shippers who tried to break the British stranglehold were victimized by Barbary pirates who, backed by France, Spain, and Morocco, stole their cargoes and demanded huge extortion fees. France, after all, had supported America during the war largely to humiliate its old enemy, England. Algiers actually declared war on America to further its demands, and sold captured Americans into slavery, where they were confined to vermin-infested dungeons, shackled and worked on treadmills, whipped, beaten, and traded in the marketplaces—hostages apparently forgotten by an impotent government at home.

In violation of the treaty, the British navy refused to help. Congress had no power to pay ransom, or to form a navy, and was unable to provide protection. Adams and Thomas Jefferson were laughed at while representing America in England and France. At home there was fear that some of the states might actually be sold, and in Europe the expectation was that the ex-colonies soon would come begging. Spain owned Florida, controlled the mouth of the Mississippi, and was eager to take on the Carolinas as well. Under intense pressure from Spain, John Jay, a brilliant statesman and secretary of foreign affairs under the Confederation, was almost forced in 1784 to bargain away America's right to use the Mississippi, which would have left the new country in ruins.

The root of the problem was that the bold men who had faced and beaten the British Empire were paralyzed by their distrust of the power of a strong central government and their fear of its becoming a tyranny; no successful republic on such a scale had existed since the days of ancient Rome, and even that had degenerated quickly into a monarchy. It therefore fell to the younger generation, raised on the blood of the Revolution, to save the United States. In particular, it fell to

James Madison and his fiery counterpart, Alexander Hamilton.

Madison and Hamilton were a study in contrast. James Madison, the son of a wealthy Virginia plantation family, had initially planned to enter the clergy. Frail and unambitious in his youth, he developed his talents only over time. He was an earnest, methodical man—devoted to the country for which his father had actively campaigned—with a calm manner that disguised an iron will and a determination to finish what he started. This cost him dearly in personal terms: early in his career, before he met and married Dolley Payne Todd, his neglected sixteen-year-old fiancée abandoned him for someone who could romance her more properly.

Elected to the Continental Congress, Madison experienced firsthand the frustrations of working for an impotent government in conflict with the selfish and often contradictory demands of the various states. His nationalism made him bitter enemies with Patrick Henry, governor of his home state of Virginia, a passionate states'-rights advocate who did not approve of Madison's efforts to create a strong Continental army. He also lost the financial support of his family, who would have preferred that he return to the plantation. Since the states often neglected to pay the salaries of their congressmen, Madison found himself in the same severe financial bind faced by many legislators. Indeed, Madison and others were often saved from poverty only by the generosity of the local Jewish moneylender, Haym Salomon, a little man with a big heart whose belief in the new country precluded any thought of accepting repayment from the destitute lawmakers.

While Madison was the even-tempered, well-connected gentleman, Alexander Hamilton was an explosive West Indian whose meteoric rise from poverty could be attributed to nothing but his own genius and drive. Growing up in the Leeward Islands, he was "the bastard brat of a Scots pedlar" and a fiery, independent woman who was the scandal of the region. A brilliant soldier, financier, and philosopher, he became lieutenant-colonel on Washington's staff in 1777, when barely into his twenties.

Where Madison failed in love, the handsome, flashy Hamilton charmed Elizabeth Schuyler and thereby married into one of New York's leading families. But his engagement didn't hinder his ongoing affairs, one of which was with Elizabeth's sister Angelica, a witty, worldly girl who had a longstanding crush on the handsome statesman. In a letter to Angelica written before he was to be married, Hamilton joked that Elizabeth would be "much less dangerous when she has a rival equal in charms to dispute the place with her. I solicit your aid."

It was in Congress that Hamilton met Madison, when the two men worked closely on a fruitless and discouraging effort to create a national revenue and pay the mutinying army in the face of states' opposition. Disgusted with the quagmire into which the country was sinking, they seized the first opportunity to work on a solution. A meeting had been called between a few states to discuss the use of the Potomac; Madison and Hamilton engineered it into a general convention, at Annapolis, for delegates from all the states to discuss the issue of commerce. They arrived to discover that only twelve delegates had shown up, their number awkwardly dwarfed by the hall in which the peace treaty with Britain had been ratified.

Rather than give in to disappointment, Hamilton drew up a ringing pamphlet calling for another, even more ambitious convention. This one, to be held at Independence Hall in Philadelphia the following May, would go far beyond commerce to address the central questions of if and how America was going to survive. It was not an easily achieved proposal. Many states, including Hamilton's home state of New York, were against a stronger national government, and many delegates were unhappy at the prospect of a long, hot summer in Philadelphia wrestling with impossible problems. But Madison and Hamilton were not to be denied. Together with two allies from Annapolis—Governor Randolph of Virginia and the wise old Scotsman James Wilson—they built support for the convention state by state. Only Rhode Island, blindly destroying itself with paper currency, refused to send delegates.

A significant absentee would be Patrick Henry, Madison's old foe, who violently opposed the convention and stayed home to organize opposition to it. Elected governor of Virginia for a time, the fiery orator who in 1775 had challenged, "Give me liberty or give me death," now directed the same salvo at the Congress. The Declaration had been Henry's goal, a separation of Virginia from England; he had no desire to see his state resubjugated to a new national master. His inflexible, radical views appeared oddly reactionary in the postwar context as he proved unwilling to abandon the patchwork of institutions left over from colonial days. A tragic, illness-ridden figure who lived to see his hour come and go, Henry ironically became the devil's advocate, unable to admit that revolution alone was not enough to secure the liberty in which he so passionately believed.

Madison did not content himself with politicking. He knew that without a solid plan to consider, the delegates would lose precious time and energy and he wanted more than just a rehash of the Articles of Confederation. Writing to Jefferson, who was serving in Paris, he asked for every book available in English, French, or Latin on natural law and the history of republican governments. Jefferson sent him two trunks full, and Madison threw himself into his studies day and night, working by candlelight to try to create out of the ghosts of the past a unique, vital reality for the future. Not that he was a novice: he had already helped the great libertarian George Mason draw up Virginia's Bill of Rights. Madison set to writing up the structure he envisioned for the government in what became known as the Virginia Plan. With various modifications, it formed the basis of the Constitution, the skeleton on which the living document was built.

The planning was progressing well. George Washington, it was assumed would be elected president of the assembly. Washington was almost universally considered the greatest living American, and Madison and Hamilton needed no less to keep the convention alive. Indeed, eighty-one-year-old Benjamin Franklin was deliberately not invited in order to avoid conflict in the election. The strategy seemed to be working—then, catastrophe. Washington declined to attend.

Washington was not against the idea of the convention, but he had intended to retire from public life. He had just declined an invitation to be honored by the Society of the Cincinnati in Philadelphia that same week; uncomfortable with presiding over this elite officers' association. Washington had several times threatened to resign unless reforms in its aristocratic doctrines were made. However, he did not wish to snub the many friends he had in the society by instead showing up for such an unlikely enterprise. The time for the convention drew near. With only a week to go, Washington still had not been persuaded. Fearing all would be lost, Madison and Hamilton at last invited Franklin to step in. On May 14, 1787, the moment arrived. Braving poor weather and muddy roads, the delegates began to assemble.

At the final hour Washington changed his mind, descending from Mount Vernon in his carriage like an Old Testament prophet. The militia—youngsters to whom he was just a legend and veterans who had actually served under his command—lined the streets as he rode through, giving him a full military salute. As the greatest soldier of the age dismounted, he was met by Ben Franklin, one of the greatest intellects. The prestige of these two grand old men, unquestioned heroes, proved vital to the success of the convention and later to the adoption of the Constitution. Heightening the sense of drama was the fact that the assembly had decided to work in secrecy, a trust that, incredibly, no one broke. Although many spoke of amending the existing articles, and although few would have admitted it, they were engaged in a coup d'etat, a peaceful, second revolution. Throughout the period of the convention the press was reduced to speculation: even the delegates' closest friends were kept in the dark. So were the antinationalists like Henry, who had boycotted the convention.

Philadelphia, the city upon which Franklin had lavished the best of his genius, was itself particularly colorful. America's largest metropolitan center, in the middle of a building boom brought on by the immigration of Irish, Germans, and Scots, Philadelphia was a mixture of raw energy and elegant high society that perfectly reflected the men who had come to decide the nations future—"an assembly of demigods," as Jefferson described them.

While most of the delegates stayed at a local inn, Washington was the guest of the richest man in America, Robert Morris, who lived in the grand manner and hosted Philadelphia's high-society affairs. Round and amiable, he was nevertheless a man of iron whose financial magic had managed to keep the wolf away from America's door in spite of all its problems. As "The Financier" of the Continental Congress, he had struggled against the disastrous flood of paper monies and tried along with his associate Gouverneur Morris, to found a central mint and a stable currency. When the disgruntled army, unpaid and in tatters, had confronted him, he and Gouverneur Morris had actually advocated the march on Congress, to demonstrate that the army's desperation (and their threat) was real. Should they fail and be forced to disband, he had said, "I will feed them." But even Morris, willing to invest his own enormous personal fortune and talents, was unable to make up for a fundamentally flawed central government. With Congress unable to raise taxes or stem its flow of debt, he had resigned, stating, "I will never be minister of injustice."

A Constitutional Add-On: Ten Amendments to Protect the Individual Rights of Citizens

Of the delegates present at the end of the convention, all but three signed the Constitution. Madison was saddened that two of these three were his old colleagues from Virginia, Governor Edmund Randolph and George Mason. They had come so far, and yet still they withheld their approval—in large part because while the document outlined the powers of government, it did not specify its limitations. The Constitution was without that ultimate guarantee of personal liberties, a bill of rights: the idea had been proposed in committee but was voted down as unnecessary. Most of the delegates reasoned that the extent of government was clearly limited by the enumeration of its powers—how could it exceed them? Eight states already had bills of rights, which were not affected by the Constitution as it stood. Perhaps Mason, as principal author of the Virginia Bill of Rights—the first in the colonies—was simply being too cautious. Yet, as before, his wisdom proved prophetic.

The absence of a bill of rights from the Constitution became the major stumbling block for subsequent ratification by the states. This issue went right to the heart of the fears many revolutionaries had about establishing a strong central government, because guaranteed rights were at the heart of the Revolution itself. The infamous Stamp and Quartering acts had been outrageous precisely because they had violated central tenets of the British Declaration of Rights: "No taxation without representation," and protection of the civilian populace from abuse by the military.

"A Bill of Rights is what the people are entitled to," declared Jefferson, "against every government on earth, general or particular."

The explicit preservation of individual liberties, the freedom from fear of the capricious or immoderate use of power by the government, were matters that few raised in the English tradition took lightly. Such freedoms had been hard won through hundreds of years of struggle, dating back at least to the summer of 1215, when King John put his forced signature to the Magna Charta on the field of Runnymede. The rights of the people, represented by an elected governing body, had been tested again and again, as the English suffered through a brutal civil war and the execution of a monarch in the seventeenth century; less than half a century later came the banishment of another. A Dutch ruler was imported only on condition that he submit to a new and much more extensive Declaration of Rights. It was a Hanoverian, George III, who broke this covenant again.

There was no way the colonists, having fought so hard to regain their rights, were going to gamble them away now. Led by Patrick Henry and joined by Mason, the anti-Federalists blasted the unamended Constitution as a model for tyranny. In vain Madison and Hamilton argued their case: it was absurd, a bill of rights would be redundant. "Why declare that things shall not be done, which there is no power to do?" Hamilton wrote in frustration. But the counterarguments were strong. It was suggested, for example, that while the state was not entitled to unreasonable search and seizure, this could be the unforeseen result of the new provision to collect taxes.

James Wilson pursued another tack in questioning the need for a bill: the very act of detailing rights would have the effect of limiting them. "Who will be bold enough to enumerate all the rights of the people? And . . . if the enumeration is not complete, everything not expressly mentioned will be presumed to be purposely omitted." Washington agreed: liberty was too dynamic to be bounded by definition. But Jefferson's words sounded a stubborn reaction. "A Bill of Rights," he declared, "is what the people are entitled to, against every government on earth, general or particular."

In the end, the Federalists realized that without the inclusion of a bill of rights, the Constitution would not be ratified. And so they promised to amend the document once the government had been elected and installed. Even so, the contest was close when it reached the states. Fistfights broke out in the Pennsylvania legislature when the Federalists forcibly kept those opposed in the hall in order to fix a quorum. In Massachusetts, out of 355 votes, the Constitution passed by only nineteen. In Virginia Madison faced the fury of Patrick Henry and the vote was uncertain—until Randolph, satisfied at last, rose and declared, "I am a friend to the Union." It passed by a mere ten votes, but pass it did.

The convention, circumventing the Continental Congress, had decided that the approval of nine states was required for ratification, and by 1788 ten had been won over. After a bitter battle fought by Hamilton and Jay against Clinton and his men, New York, the "eleventh pillar," finally went along by a margin of three votes. James Wilson wrote to his wife: "Last night they fired thirteen cannon . . . , over the funeral of the Confederation, and this morning they saluted the new government with eleven cannon." North Carolina and Rhode Island, still committed to local paper currencies, refused to ratify but were not long in changing direction.

The Federalists kept their promise. In his inaugural address, penned by Madison, Washington asked for suggested amendments. Out of the hundreds of submissions, Madison narrowed the field to seventeen, working in the Congress with the help of Jefferson, Mason, and others. Twelve amendments were adopted by the Congress and sent out to the states. The first two dealt with congressional details and were voted down; the other ten were adopted. Generally based on Mason's bill for Virginia, the amendments fell into four categories: the first was essentially a Jeffersonian restatement of the "open society"; the second, third, and fourth grew directly out of the military and political struggles of recent history and prevented military infringement on the rights and privacy of the people; the fifth through eighth went back to the "Law of the Land," passed down from the Magna Charta, and protected the rights of the individual from abuse by the legal system; the ninth and tenth disposed of Wilson's objections, by guaranteeing to the people and the states any and all rights not expressly curtailed by the Constitution.

As it turns out, the colonists' wary insistence on explicit protection of individual liberties proved to be brilliantly farsighted; throughout our history people have found refuge from injustice in the provisions that were then laid out. Nor did the impulse toward freedom stop with the first ten amendments. As the late Justice William O. Douglas suggested, the Bill of Rights now also includes the thirteenth, fourteenth, fifteenth, and nineteenth amendments, which abolish slavery and guarantee citizenship, the right to vote, and equal protection under the law regardless of race, color, or sex. "Our Bill of Rights . . . subjects all departments of government to a rule of law and sets boundaries beyond which no official may go," observed Douglas. "It emphasizes that in this country man walks with dignity and without fear, that he need not grovel before an all-powerful government."

—R.U.R.

Morris's former counsel and another key figure at the convention was James Wilson of Pennsylvania. A tall, erudite Scotsman, Wilson came to the New World at the age of 23 to seek his fortune, became a lawyer, and was a signer of the Declaration. He, like Morris, had experienced firsthand the anger of the mob when his own house was attacked. Known as the "Fort Wilson Riot," the attack was spurred on by impoverished radicals resentful of what they viewed as the vested interests of the lawyers and bankers. Rallying at a nearby tavern, the Mob descended while Wilson and about thirty of his friends, barricaded inside, sent for help. Before the militia could arrive, one man was dead on either side. The incident was a sign that the law itself was under fire, and it made Wilson one of the most committed delegates at the convention.

Washington, as everyone had expected, was elected president of the assembly. Madison, working behind the scenes, had Edmund Randolph introduce his Virginia Plan. The hard work had begun. Although everyone in the company was civil, strong animosities, which often went beyond difference of opinion, were present. Essentially, four sets of difficulties had to be overcome: the conflict in interests between the larger, more populous states and the smaller, more vulnerable ones; the balance of power between the nation as a whole and the individual states; the issue of slavery; and the creation of an executive branch strong enough to be effective and yet incapable of hardening into a dictatorship. In every instance the convention was exploring uncharted waters.

In every instance the convention was exploring uncharted waters.

The Virginia Plan ran into immediate opposition from small states, both northern and southern, because it called for representation in Congress, whether composed of one house or two, based on population. The existing Congress instead gave one vote to each state. The idea of a popular national government, even then, was so daring, so untried, that it took a great leap of the imagination to see how it could work. Furthermore, such a system would mean a permanent underdog position for the less populous states. The southern delegates proposed that if this plan were adopted, they would accept it only if slaves were counted as part of the population, even though slaves had no vote. The small northern states objected because they feared domination by always-devious New York, and formed an unnatural alliance with the slave states.

The chief spokesmen for these interests and Madison's most vocal and aggressive opponents, were Luther Martin of Maryland and William Paterson of New Jersey. Martin had arrived in a storm of doubt, continued throughout in a storm of discontent, and left at the end in a storm of disgust. This stocky, untidy figure, with his loud voice and back-country manners, was the sore thumb of the convention, sure to voice opposition to anything he believed threatened the self-determination of small communities, whether it involved taxes, representation, or legal jurisdiction. From a poor, rural background, Martin had become rich through his talents as an attorney, but unlike Hamilton he had no aspirations to aristocracy. He was the shrewd country lawyer, distrustful of national politicians, and he fought tirelessly for the preservation of states' rights. Martin had married the daughter of a man Jefferson had accused of slaughtering the family of a friendly Indian chief; Martin never forgave Jefferson, using his name as a curse. He was also a lusty drinker who could distress and astonish his colleagues and clients by getting rip-roaring drunk only a few hours before a trial and then showing up and giving a masterful performance.

Paterson was more genteel. Born in Ireland but educated at Princeton, he had been in all the right places and met all the right people. He was "a man of great modesty, with looks that bespeak talents of no great extent, but whose powers break in on you." Paterson's motives in opposing Madison's efforts were not entirely selfless, since after the Revolution he had invested heavily in undervalued, confiscated loyalist properties. Under the Treaty of Peace, these holdings were to be returned lawfully to their former owners, something only a strong national government could enforce. Together he and Martin introduced a proposal to counter Madison's, the New Jersey Plan, aimed at forming a federation more in keeping with the existing articles and preserving a great deal of state autonomy—but it was too little, too late, and was rejected.

While the New Jersey Plan had failed, Martin and Paterson's arguments against centralization had succeeded in putting Madison's nationalist Virginia Plan in jeopardy. Hamilton saw they were losing ground fast, and tensions arose between him and Madison. Using his own considerable skills as a writer and orator, he took the surprising step of drafting yet another proposal only this one was for a national government so strong that the states would have almost no say whatsoever. The Congress would be elected for life, and it in turn would elect a president-for-life whose power approached that of a monarch. The convention, shocked by the extremism of Hamilton's proposal, voted it down. It had very likely been a ploy. The delegates returned with renewed appreciation to the Virginia Plan, which now seemed reasonably moderate. Martin again responded with a long and impassioned plea for states' rights, but his moment had passed. He and Paterson were forced into a position they held to the end, that of embittered nay-sayers.

Although Hamilton had helped achieve a tactical victory his relations with Madison were still strained. He had also been continuously opposed in his efforts by the other New York delegates, men hand-picked by his enemy, George Clinton, governor of New York. Clinton was a huge brawler of a man, a pork-barrel politician determined to keep New York independent (and under his thumb), and was personally antagonistic to Hamilton. He had prevented John Jay, Madison and Hamilton's ally and partner in writing the *Federalist* papers, from being a delegate to the convention. Although he could not bar Hamilton, given his role at Annapolis, Clinton hamstrung him by sending two violently antinationalist delegates to accompany him. Respected for his force and geniality, Clinton also had a brutal streak, and he evidenced his contempt for the national government by decimating a local tribe of Iroquois Indians in disregard of a treaty they had signed with Congress in 1784. When Clinton's delegates withdrew in protest from the assembly, New York was left without an effective vote. At the end of June, tired and disgusted, Hamilton left the convention and returned home to be with his wife and resume his neglected law practice.

His withdrawal did not improve the mood of the assembly, who would all have loved to follow his example. The summer was hot and sticky and everyone was anxious to get back on track, frustrated by the long and fruitless debates. Tensions were running so high, in fact, that Franklin stunned the company by suggesting each session begin with a prayer to God for help. The suggestion was not taken up, but the point was made; with or without prayer, there was business to be done. Over the Independence Day hiatus, Franklin helped Roger Sherman and his Connecticut delegation forge the Great Compromise, without which there would have been no Constitution: Congress would have two houses, one of which would represent the general population, and one of which would represent the states in equal measure. Madison was not happy with it, fearing the parochialism of the states, but it was compromise or lose the whole fight. To his pleasant surprise, after winning this victory, many of his former opponents from the smaller states outdid one another in working for a stronger national government.

Over the Independence Day hiatus, Franklin helped forge the Great Compromise, without which there would have been no Constitution.

A major obstacle overcome, it was decided that a short break would help restore energy and good humor to the assembly. With the exception of a small committee assigned to record what had been accomplished so far, the delegates took a ten day vacation. Washington and fellow delegate Gouverneur Morris decided to go fishing at Valley Forge. There, in the heat of the summer, among the decaying remains of fortifications, they reminisced about the fateful, freezing winter of a decade before.

In the arguments that followed this peaceful interlude, one can already sense the coming storm of the Civil War. The delegates returned to find their progress drafted up, with an unexpected addition. In the drafting committee, the South Carolina delegation had inserted a provision prohibiting any form of taxation on imports, or exports, including slaves. It was a direct move to maintain the slave trade, something most of the northern and middle states had abolished, and was particularly significant since it had implications for the spread of slavery throughout the unchartered western provinces.

One of the Massachusetts delegates, Rufus King, violently objected to having slavery actually codified into the structure of the new government. After all, even the feeble Continental Congress had managed to forbid the spread of slavery above the Ohio River, acting independently on the Northwest Ordinance just the month before. Gouverneur Morris, a Pennsylvanian of Huguenot ancestry—usually one of the most charming and politic of the delegates—stood up on his peg leg and in an uncharacteristic rage gave one of the most stirring antislavery speeches on record, eighty years ahead of its time. "It is a nefarious institution," he cried. "It is the curse of Heaven on the states where it prevails!" Even Martin added his thunder to this protest. But the South, already in financial straits and almost totally dependent on a slave population that often exceeded one third of the total census, was not to be denied. In the sweltering August weather, the majority of the delegates, impatient to move on to other issues, agreed to a fence-straddling compromise. The issue of slave ownership was essentially left up to the individual states, with restrictions imposed on its spread into free western territories, partial inclusion of nonvoting slaves in determining the population census allowed, and a stipulation ending the importation of slaves after 1808.

In retrospect, the inability to define a solid position in regard to slavery and the commercial conflicts between North and South was perhaps the greatest failing of the convention, putting off a confrontation that would only grow worse until it eventually erupted in war. George Mason, as always the standard-bearer for individual liberty, sounded a prophetic warning: "Providence punishes national sins by national calamities."

The challenges of working out an executive and an independent judiciary put the talents of the convention to the test. How could a presidency be created that effectively administered the laws, provided military leadership, and offered a unified political vision without instituting a dictatorship? There was no precedent for it: every previous historical effort to consolidate power in one or a few men had led to disaster. Debate on how the president should be elected was lengthy: direct popular vote was technically unfeasible, and no one trusted the state legislatures. Finally, following a brilliant suggestion from Wilson, a new democratic process—the electoral college—was invented, striking a balance between the demands of the states and the rights of the voters.

The convention was aided in mid-August by the return of Hamilton, who, his temper restored, was anxious to contribute. But it was Washington's presence that was essential. As the assembly hammered out the powers and limitations of the executive, they knew full well who the first man to fill the office would be. More than Hamilton's brilliant rhetoric, it was their personal trust in Washington that led to the creation of a much stronger executive than any of them, particularly, the states' righters, had expected—a true Commander in Chief. They modeled the presidency on Washington, and Washington was to serve as the model for all future presidents. At the same time they worked out the structure and responsibilities of the judiciary branch, a less threatening and hence less divisive issue for this gathering of lawyers.

At last, a full four months after they had begun, the document was complete. It was given to Gouverneur Morris, a magnificent stylist, to be translated into the elegant language that has resounded throughout our history. A brief debate ensued on whether or nor to put the various parts of it to Congress or to the individual states for ratification, but the idea was dismissed. The document had been written in secrecy, without consulting the Confederation or the separate legislatures, and it would be presented for adoption as it stood, whole, a new beginning for a troubled land. On September 17, the final vote taken, the Constitution was adopted by the assembly and was signed by the majority of the delegates.

Franklin, the patriarch of the convention, wrote the stirring closing speech, which he asked fellow Pennsylvanian James Wilson, with his genteel burr, to read. As the delegates began to file out of Independence Hall, their great labor ended, Franklin turned his gaze to a painting of a sun at the back of Washington's chair. "I have," he said to those around him, "often and often in the course of the session ... looked at that behind the President without being able to tell whether it was rising or setting. But now at length I have the happiness to know that it is a rising and not setting sun."

The United States Constitution, celebrating its two hundredth birthday this year, is regarded with almost religious reverence by most Americans. While it makes no claim to divine authorship, we turn to it for guidance and answers with the same devotion the Greeks once showed their oracles at Delphi and Olympia. It is the shrine containing the best wisdom of our best men; our sense of what is right or wrong has become virtually indistinguishable from what is, or is not, constitutional.

Oracles are mystical creatures, and so perhaps it is not remarkable how little most of us know about how and why the Constitution came to be written, about what America was in the tumultuous decade between the Declaration of Independence and the drafting of this great document. Our Constitution seems to have come down to us from the mountain like the tablets of Moses, written in blazing letters to announce the doctrines we now equate with enlightened civilization. And yet it was, and is, a human document, and was anything but a natural consequence of the Revolution. It was the brainchild of extraordinary men living in extraordinary times, an astonishing, unique compromise among contending ideologies, a mosaic patterned to bring humane order to the fragmentation the war had left in its wake. It was, in fact, the manifesto of a second revolution, whose vital momentum continues to affect us to this day. The convention in Philadelphia that long, hot summer two centuries ago was a gamble against seemingly impossible odds on the part of a few dedicated, desperate patriots, a now-or-never move that John Adams described as "the greatest single effort of national deliberation that the world has ever seem."

Chapter 2 Exercise

Identify and discuss the four difficulties that confronted the delegates at the Convention.

Why was George Washington's role so crucial in the creation of the Constitution?

PART III

Separation of Powers and Federalism

CHAPTER 3

Separated Powers

The Federalist #51

James Madison

In Federalist #51, Madison makes the case for separation of powers. In an effort to preserve liberty, "you must first enable the government to control the governed; and in the next place oblige it to control itself." The federal government would be limited precisely because the branches possessed roughly equal power. In this way no one institution could act without the support of the other.

To what expedient, then, shall we finally resort, for maintaining in practice the necessary partition of power among the several departments as laid down in the Constitution? The only answer that can be given is that as all these exterior provisions are found to be inadequate the defect must be supplied, by so contriving the interior structure of the government as that its several constituent parts may, by their mutual relations, be the means of keeping each other in their proper places. Without presuming to undertake a full development of this important idea I will hazard a few general observations which may perhaps place it in a clearer light, and enable us to form a more correct judgment of the principles and structure of the government planned by the convention.

In order to lay a due foundation for that separate and distinct exercise of the different powers of government, which to a certain extent is admitted on all hands to be essential to the preserva-tion of liberty, it is evident that each department should have a will of its own; and consequently should be so constituted that the members of each should have as little agency as possible in the appointment of the members of the others. Were this principle rigorously adhered to, it would require that all the appointments for the supreme executive, legislative, and judiciary magistracies should be drawn from the same fountain of authority, the people, through chan-nels having no communication whatever with one another. Perhaps such a plan of constructing the several departments would be less difficult in practice than it may in contemplation appear. Some difficulties, however, and some additional expense would attend the execution of it. Some deviations, therefore, from the principle must be admitted. In the constitution of the judiciary department in particular, it might be inexpedient to insist rigorously on the principle: first, because peculiar qualifications being essential in the members, the primary consideration ought to be to select that mode of choice which best secures these qualifications; second, because the permanent tenure by which the appointments are held in that department must soon destroy all sense of dependence on the authority conferring them.

It is equally evident that the members of each department should be as little dependent as possible on those of the others for the emoluments annexed to their offices. Were the executive magistrate, or the judges, not independent of the legislature in this particular, their independence in every other would be merely nominal.

But the great security against a gradual concentration of the several powers in the same department consists in giving to those who administer each department the necessary constitutional means and personal motives to resist encroachments of the others. The provision for defense must in this, as in all other cases, be made commensurate to the danger of attack. Ambition must be made to counteract ambition. The interest of the man must be connected with the constitutional rights of the place. It may be a reflection on human nature that such devices should be necessary to control the abuses of government. But what is government itself but the greatest of all reflections on human nature? If men were angels, no government would be necessary. If angels were to govern men, neither external nor internal controls on government would be necessary. In framing a government which is to be administered by men over men, the great difficulty lies in this: you must first enable the government to control the governed; and in the next place oblige it to control itself. A dependence on the people is, no doubt, the primary control on the government; but experience has taught mankind the necessity of auxiliary precautions.

This policy of supplying, by opposite and rival interests, the defect of better motives, might be traced through the whole system of human affairs, private as well as public. We see it particularly displayed in all the subordinate distributions of power, where the constant aim is to divide and arrange the several offices in such a manner as that each may be a check on the other—that the private interest of every individual may be a sentinel over the public rights. These inventions of prudence cannot be less requisite in the distribution of the supreme powers of the State.

But it is not possible to give to each department an equal power of self-defense. In republican government, the legislative authority necessarily predominates. The remedy for this inconveniency is to divide the legislature into different branches; and to render them, by different modes of election and different principles of action, as little connected with each other as the nature of their common functions and their common dependence on the society will admit. It may even be necessary to guard against dangerous encroachments by still further precautions. As the weight of the legislative authority requires that it should be thus divided, the weakness of the executive may require, on the other hand, that it should be fortified. An absolute negative on the legislature appears, at first view, to be the natural defense with which the executive magistrate should be armed. But perhaps it would be neither altogether safe nor alone sufficient. On ordinary occasions it might not be exerted with the requisite firmness, and on extraordinary occasions it might be perfidiously abused. May not this defect of an absolute negative be supplied by some qualified connection between this weaker branch of the stronger department, by which the latter may be led to support the constitutional rights of the former, without being too much detached from the rights of its own department?

If the principles on which these observations are founded be just, as I persuade myself they are, and they be applied as a criterion to the several State constitutions, and to the federal Constitution, it will be found that if the latter does not perfectly correspond with them, the former are infinitely less able to bear such a test.

There are, moreover, two considerations particularly applicable to the federal system of America, which place that system in a very interesting point of view.

First. In a single republic, all the power surrendered by the people is submitted to the administration of a single government; and the usurpations are guarded against by a division of the government into distinct and separate departments. In the compound republic of America, the power surrendered by the people is first divided between two distinct governments, and then the portion allotted to each subdivided among distinct and separate departments. Hence a double security arises to the rights of the people. The different governments will control each other, at the same time that each will be controlled by itself.

Second. It is of great importance in a republic not only to guard the society against the oppression of its rulers, but to guard one part of the society against the injustice of the other part. Different interests necessarily exist in different classes of citizens. If a majority be united by a common interest, the rights of the minority will be insecure. There are but two methods of providing against this evil: the one by creating a will in the community independent of the majority—that is, of the society itself; the other, by comprehending in the society so many separate descriptions of citizens as will render an unjust combination of a majority of the whole very improbable, if not impracticable. The first method prevails in all governments possessing an hereditary or self-appointed authority. This, at best, is but a precarious security; because a power independent of the society may as well espouse the unjust views of the major as the rightful interests of the minor party, and may possibly be turned against both parties. The second method will be exemplified in the federal republic of the United States. Whilst all authority in it will be derived from and dependent on the society, the society itself will be broken into so many parts, interests and classes of citizens, that the rights of individuals, or of the minority, will be in little danger from interested combinations of the majority. In a free government the security for civil rights must be the same as that for religious rights. It consists in the one case in the multiplicity of interests, and in the other in the multiplicity of sects. The degree of security in both cases will depend on the number of interests and sects; and this may be presumed to depend on the extent of country and number of people comprehended under the same government. This view of the subject must particularly recommend a proper federal system to all the sincere and considerate friends of republican government, since it shows that in exact proportion as the territory of the Union may be formed into more circumscribed Confederacies, or States, oppressive combinations of a majority will be facilitated; the best security, under the republican forms, for the rights of every class of citizen, will be diminished; and consequently the stability and independence of some member of the government, the only other security; must be proportionally increased. Justice is the end of government. It is the end of civil society. It ever has been and ever will be pursued until it be obtained, or until liberty be lost in the pursuit. In a society under the forms of which the stronger faction can readily unite and oppress the weaker, anarchy may as truly be said to reign as in a state of nature, where the weaker individual is not secured against the violence of the stronger; and as, in the latter state, even the stronger individuals are prompted, by the uncertainty of their condition, to submit to a government which may protect the weak as well as themselves; so, in the former state, will the more powerful factions or parties be gradually induced, by a like motive, to wish for a government which will protect all parties, the weaker as well as the more powerful. It can be little doubted that if the State of Rhode Island was separated from the Confederacy and left to itself, the insecurity of rights under the popular form of government within such narrow limits would be displayed by such reiterated oppressions of factious majorities that some power altogether independent of the people would soon be called for by the voice of the very factions whose misrule had proved the necessity of it. In the extended republic of the United States, and among the great variety of interests, parties, and sects which it embraces, a coalition of a majority of the whole society could seldom take place on any other principles than those of justice and the general good; whilst there being thus less danger to a minor from the will of a major party, there must be less pretext, also, to provide for the security of the former, by introducing into the government a will not dependent on the latter, or, in other words, a will independent of the society itself. It is no less certain than it is important, notwithstanding the contrary opinions which have been entertained, that the larger the society, provided it lie within a practicable sphere, the more duly capable it will be of self-government. And happily for the *republican cause,* the practicable sphere may be carried to a very great extent by a judicious modification and mixture of the *federal principle.*

Chapter 3 Exercise

What does Madison's phrase "Ambition must be made to counteract ambition" have to do with the structure of our federal government?

Madison believed that the legislative branch would dominate the other federal institutions. Why? What was his remedy for this potential problem?

CHAPTER 4

Checks, Balances, Equilibrium

A Self-Correcting System:
The Constitution of the United States

Martin Landau

Martin Landau observed that the framers of the Constitution must have been Newtonians: The political system can be conceived much like a natural system and Newton's 3rd law was "action and reaction, thrust and counter thrust, or what we call checks and balances." Landau proposes that the Constitution provides for a self-regulating and self-correcting system that exhibits reliability, stability, and adaptability. These attributers, over some 200 years, have overcome many obstacles and made for a strong, though inefficient, system of government.

The great English philosopher, Alfred North Whitehead, once remarked, "I know of only two occasions in history when the people in power did what needed to be done about as well as you can imagine its being possible. One was the framing of your American Constitution." (His other example was the reign of Augustus Caesar.) The framers, Whitehead added, were able statesmen with good ideas which they incorporated "without trying to particularize too explicitly how they should be put into effect."

Years before he became president of the United States, Woodrow Wilson, in reflecting on the durability of the Constitution, also observed its generalized character. It did little more than lay down a foundation in principle, Wilson remarked; it was not a complete system; it took none but the first steps. The Constitution, he continued, provided with all possible brevity for the establishment of a government having three distinct branches: executive, legislative and judicial. It vested executive power in the presidency,

Reprinted with permission from "A Self-Correcting System: The Constitution of the United States," by Martin Landau, from *This Constitution: A Bicentennial Chronicle*, Summer 1986, published by Project '87 of the American Political Science Association (APSA) and the American Historical Association (AHA).

for whose election and inauguration it made careful provision, and whose powers it defined with succinct clarity; it granted specifically enumerated powers to Congress, outlined the organization of its two houses, provided for the election of its members and regulated both their numbers and the manner of their election; it established a Supreme Court with ample authority to interpret the Constitution, and it prescribed the procedures to govern appointments and tenure.

At this point, Wilson noted, the organizational work of the Constitution ended and "the fact that it [did] nothing more [was] its chief strength." Had it gone beyond such elementary provisions, it would have lost elasticity and adaptability. Its ability to endure, to survive, was directly attributable to its simplicity.

There is strong ground for such belief. State constitutions, notoriously complicated, cluttered, and rigid, have come and gone—tossed away as outmoded, inelastic, and maladaptive instruments. Since 1789, there have been some two hundred state constitutional conventions, one, it seems, for every year of our history. This should not surprise us when we observe that the average size of our state constitutions is ten times that of the national, the movement toward simplification notwithstanding. But the national Constitution, framed for a simple society marked by doubtful unity and fearsome external threat, now orders a world that would appear as science fiction to its designers. Where states have had to scrap their constitutions five, seven, even ten times, the nation's remains intact.

Despite Wilson's admiration of the simple brevity of the Constitution, he wondered about the future of a governmental system in which "nothing is direct." "Authority," he stated, "is perplexingly subdivided and distributed, and responsibility has to be hunted down in out-of-the-way corners."

In this sentence we have the crux of an unending stream of criticism which remains vigorous to this date. One frequently hears that separation of powers has resulted in continuous struggle between president and Congress, too often leading to deadlock; that the decline of

Congress and the rise of an "imperial presidency" is ample testimony to the failure of checks and balances—a failure further intensified by a Supreme Court which remains beyond the reach of Congress, president, and the public. So too has federalism failed. It has fractured and fragmented the nation, nurtured the parochialism of local interests, furthered the imbalances of society, and subverted efforts to mount coordinated national programs. In the decline of the states and the ascendancy of national power, little of the original design remains. And beyond this, the staggered electoral system has prevented the majority from controlling its government or ousting one it does not want.

Whatever their logical consistency, these are frequent and familiar criticisms that derive from a variety of sources. They give rise to all sorts of remedial proposals from a fixed single term for the presidency to a parliamentary system. They abound today, and their proponents are prominent public figures who delight in telling us that no other modern government on the European continent has used the American Constitution as its model. Because of distinctive ethnic and regional problems, some have employed the principle of federalism but none has been impressed with the cumbersome and conflict-prone separation of powers. The issue, publicized in the media, is the "ungovernability" of the system: separation of power breaks down into stalemate, delay, nonfeasance, even malfeasance. What captures critics is the apparent inefficiencies of our governing institutions.

But it would do us all well to remember Justice Brandeis' injunction that the Constitution was not a design for efficiency. Nor is it by any means as simple as Wilson thought. In the brevity of the seven articles which established the government, there is contained an organizational logic that we are only now beginning to fathom. Separation of powers and federalism as we understand these concepts, do not quite cover the organizational principles involved. But they are critical elements in all "self-regulating" and "high reliability" systems—which is what the Constitution established.

Self-Regulating Systems

Before turning directly to this concept, it is important to note that to the eighteenth century, the system of mechanics formulated by Isaac Newton was not simply a scientific theory. Indeed, it had become a cosmological formula so powerful as to constitute "an infallible world outlook." So it was that the English poet, Alexander Pope, could write, "Nature and nature's laws lay hid in night, God said, 'Let Newton be,' and all was light."

Whatever their political differences, those who wrote the Constitution were Newtonians. With few exceptions, they thought the governmental system they were designing was in accord with nature's way. And nature's way, so elegantly stated in Newton's Third Law, was action and reaction, thrust and counter-thrust, or what we call checks and balances. There are, John Adams had written, three branches in any government and "they have an unalterable foundation in nature": "to constitute a single body with all power, *without any counterpoise, balance, or equilibrium* is to violate the laws of nature" but "to hold powers in balance is a self-evident truth."

This was the ideal struck in Philadelphia—a government that by its natural properties minimized the risk of human error. The true principle of government, Hamilton declared, is "to give a *perfect proportion and balance to its parts,* and the power you give it will never affect your security." And to Madison, a "natural government" was such that "its several constituent parts may, by their mutual relations, be the means of keeping each other in their proper places," of regulating and controlling each other.

So too did this image comprehend federalism. A "natural" government, after all, was a transcript of nature and nature was a machine. Look at this world, David Hume wrote-"You will find it to be nothing but one great machine, subdivided into an infinite number of lesser machines ... adjusted to each other with an accuracy which ravishes into admiration all men who have ever contemplated them." Look at these United States, Jefferson might have written, one great government subdivided into lesser governments, adjusted to each other with an accuracy. . . . What he did write was:

> In time all these [states] as well as the central government, like the planets revolving around their common sun, acting and acted upon according to their respective weights and distances, will produce that beautiful equilibrium on which our Constitution is founded, and which I believe it will exhibit to the world in a degree of perfection, unexampled but in the planetary system itself.

Balance, equilibrium, stability: these were the goals the framers of the Constitution sought. Once, in exasperation, Walter Lippmann asked: "Is there in all the world a more plain-spoken attempt to contrive an automatic governor, a machine that would not need to take human nature into account?" To Lippmann, a noted political analyst, government was not a problem in mechanics, and its solutions were not to be found in a balance of forces. Such a balance, he held, leads not to stability, but to paralysis. But a ship on the high seas and a jet in the sky are stable systems. They constantly change in velocity and vector, yet they remain in equilibrium.

There are stable systems that are self-regulating. They can prevent error and they can correct error; some are able to repair themselves even as damage occurs. Generally addressed as "cybernetic," their governing principle is "feedback." By cycling back a portion of their output, they are able to avoid and suppress sharp pendulum-like swings. What is fed back regulates and stabilizes the system. This is often referred to as "feedback stabilization." That there is a striking resemblance between "checks and balances" and "feedback stabilization" was observed some years ago by the noted scientist, John R. Platt.

In a stabilization or self-regulating system, internal checks are introduced to prevent error, stress, or threat from so building that the system breaks down suddenly and dangerously. Protection is acquired, as Hamilton would phrase it, by proportioning the system so that its parts balance each other, so that they regulate each other. In modern parlance, we refer to "feedback loops" which enable parts to work against each other and even against the whole. Counter-forces of this type prevent discontinuities, wild oscillation, and rapid fluctuation. Wholesale breakdowns, due either to extreme mutability or rigidity, are thereby avoided. This is a type of self or internal regulation which permits stable operations even as the system changes.

In the constitutional design, Platt suggested, "the idea was to set up, at every critical point . . . , some kind of equilibrium between opposing interests . . . so as to have a steady pressure against either the excesses or defects of policy into which governments were likely to fall." Or, as James Madison put it, "to control itself," a government's "interior structure" must be so arranged that the relationship of the parts regulates the whole. This is the function of checks and balances or, in Platt's language, negative feedback.

In a self-regulating system, any number of devices are employed to maintain and insure stability of operation. Because a system constantly and inevitably faces unexpected and uncertain conditions which generate a wide variety of problems, its repertoire of response must be rather extensive. Accordingly, self-regulating systems are designed in terms of different time constants, different response levels, and brakes and accelerators—along with its multiple feedback linkages. There are problems that demand rapid action. There are others which require careful and deliberate consideration. Disturbances to a system are not all alike: they will vary in intensity, character, cost, and duration. Hence a range of time constants, of schedules and calendars, each having its own place in the system, is required.

There are also problems that directly affect the whole and must be dealt with at the systemic level. Others are, by their nature, best handled at intermediate levels. Still others, of lesser magnitude, engage only a part of the system. Decision and choice points, thus, must be located at places most appropriate to the problem. And there are times when it is necessary to slow action, or to speed action. For such circumstances, brakes and accelerators are necessary. The idea is to enable the system to act as a whole even as it distributes and differentiates authority to decide, and to produce a powerful capacity to respond to a multitude of different types of problems simultaneously.

Taken as a whole, an organization of this sort does appear to be "perplexingly subdivided and distributed" and it certainly looks messy. But a variety of time constants, differential response levels, brakes and accelerators, and multiple forms of feedback are precisely the elements that protect against dangerous fluctuations and permit a deliberate change process which insures stability.

These safeguards are all to be found in the Constitution. They were placed there by men who knew what they were doing, and explained what they were doing. One needs only to read *The Federalist* papers. There we find explanations of the different systems of recruitment, staggered tenure, separation and division of power, concurrent authorities, varieties of decision rules, multiplicity of choice points—all arranged in such a manner as to produce networks of internal control. These failed only once; in the years of the Civil War. The repair was costly but it was affected. And since then no threat to the system was ever allowed to amplify to the point where it threatened stability. It is a plain fact that neither war, nor depression, nor natural calamity, has ever been able to shatter its self-correcting arrangements.

It is also striking to observe the number of cybernetic theorists who see analogy in the American system of checks and balances. The anthropologist Gregory Bateson and the psychiatrist Jurgen Reusch, both concerned to avoid wild swings in the interest of stable development, saw the variety of "cross-overs" in the American system as constraints and accelerators which combine to regulate "the rate or direction" of over-all change. And C. R. Dechert, in *The Development of Cybernetics* tells us:

> The founding fathers of the United States wanted the legislature sensitive to public opinion, so they introduced a House of Representatives elected biannually on the

basis of population. But they did not want the decision process too sensitive to public opinion, so they introduced a Senate elected on a different basis for a different term of office whose concurrence is necessary to legislation. In order to introduce further stability into the system they decoupled the legislative from the executive branch and introduced an independent control element in the form of a Supreme Court. The inherent stability of the system has been proved over the past 175 years.

We like to tell our students that the Constitution was designed to endure, to outlast human deficiencies: that it is a system which "by its own internal contrivances" regulates itself. There are times, to be sure, when its pace is maddeningly slow. But in the main, it has met traumatic assaults and threats without much loss of systemic stability. There are many ways to account for this but whatever the theory employed, it remains the fact, in Platt's words, that the constitutional designers understood the principles of a self-regulating system far better than our contemporary political philosophers. Nor were they oblivious to the problem of reliability.

Redundancy and Reliability

Theories of organization frequently involve reference to *peaked* and *flat* systems. Peaked systems are hierarchies. There is only one central decision point, one channel of authority, one official or legitimate communication system. Each component operates in lock-step dependence, part of a single chain. Policy is determined at the top and prescribes the behavior of each subordinate unit.

The Constitution provides for a flat organization. There are many decision points, many authority centers, and many communications channels—all mandated. The entire system is constructed on the basis of duplication and overlap, and each major component—the executive, legislative, and judicial—has independent authority. Policy is determined through negotiation and constitutes an agreement by parties of equal standing.

It is the flat character of the government that Woodrow Wilson despaired of. And this is the property of the system that has been subjected to unceasing criticism. We have already rehearsed the argument: it results in conflict, deadlock, lack of accountability, and robs us of a dynamic and vital decision center capable of quick and decisive action. For the last sixty years there have been countless reorganization proposals to "peak" the system, to locate more and more decision authority in the presidency—even beyond that which naturally accrued to the office as the United States became the United State. Until the advent of the "imperial presidency" and the excesses of Watergate, there were few voices in support of the flat system designed so long ago—a design that is also remarkable in its anticipation of the theory of redundancy.

Suppose there is a structure (or process or channel) which will fail one time in a hundred. What would the probability of simultaneous failure be for two such systems—each independent of the other? What would the probability of failure be for three systems; for four, etc.? For two, the chance of failure would be 1 in 10,000; for three, 1 in 1,000,000; for four, 1 in 100,000,000. This fact, the product rule of probability, lies at the foundation of the theory of redundancy, which is a theory of system reliability. Applied properly, it lessens the risk of failure and protects against the injurious effects of major errors and malfunctions. Its cardinal element is simple repetition or duplication.

And its basic assumptions are Madisonian—that mankind is fallible—not good, not bad—just prone to error. It agrees that "if men were angels" or "if angels governed men," no special safeguards or auxiliary precautions would be necessary. The theory of redundancy simply accepts the obvious limitations of any and all systems—political, economic, social, physical, natural, and artificial—by treating their parts, no matter how perfect, *as risky actors*. The theory focuses on the whole and asks one paramount question: is it possible to construct a system that is more reliable, more perfect, less prone to failure than even the most faithful of its components? When we set this question against that time-honored maxim—a chain is no stronger than its weakest link—its full import is made clear. The theory tells us that a chain can not only be made stronger than its weakest link, it can be made stronger than its strongest link.

It has generally escaped notice but this is the problem that much of *The Federalist* papers dealt with. "As long as the reason of man continues fallible," as long "as enlightened statesmen will not always be at the helm," how can we devise a government that will withstand gross malfunction as it continues to serve its purposes? The answer: by so organizing it that when some parts fail *they do not and can not automatically cause the failure of others*. The idea is to provide a system with multiple channels, independent of each other, at those points where failure can be disastrous. Where this type of redundancy is incorporated into a design, the odds against total breakdown rise by many times. The failure of one part cannot and does not irreparably damage the whole. There are alternative pathways, backups, which move the entity toward failsafe. In real machines, we have learned to insure reliability through the redundancy of simple duplication, as in a power-grid, a 747, and the dual braking system of our cars. And, intuitively, we follow the same principle when we seek a second opinion in a threatening medical situation.

The founders constructed what was, and still must be, the most redundant government in the world. They did more than introduce internal balances and controls: they "wired" the system in parallel at every crucial choice point. There is no unity of command and authority: there is no monopoly of power. The system is flat. And for each person there are, at the least, two governments—state and national, each separate and independent. There are two constitutions, two executives, two legislatures, two systems of law, two judiciaries. There are two bills of rights, two networks of checks and balances; two representation systems, and there is more. For

apart from the redundancy of duplication, manifested in federalism, there is also the redundancy of checks and balances; i.e., of "overlapping jurisdictions."

In the event of damage, overlapping systems can expand their jurisdictions and "take over" when the functions of others have been lost or impaired. There are indeed limits which vary with the type of system, but an inherent protective potential is thereby established. In the case of the Constitution, our three basic branches are designed to overlap. They resist mutually exclusive jurisdictions. And they expand and contract. Scholars have for years spoken of the "cyclical" character of intragovernmental arrangements, of "pendulum" swings—frequently pointing to these as adaptive responses. The "uncertain content" (jurisdiction) of the three branches of government does not allow any one of them to sit still. If one weakens or fails, the other can affect a partial takeover. And the same holds for the national and state governments.

A system thus can sustain failure that, in the absence of overlapping jurisdictions, would destroy it. Once, on the floor of the Senate, Senator Mike Mansfield ... warned his colleagues that their refusal to act on a critical issue would not prevail: "It is clear that when one road to this end fails, others will unfold as indeed they have. ... If the process is ignored in legislative channels, it will not be blocked in other channels—in the executive branch and the courts." This has been the pattern of much of our history.

It is a history that confirms Whitehead's judgment. The constitutional system works as a "self-regulating" and "self-correcting" organization exhibiting a reliability, stability, and adaptability that has continually overcome its deepest strains. We like to say that ours is the oldest written Constitution in the world—yet it remains a striking novelty. Marked by a redundancy of law, of channel and code, of command and authority, the whole has been stronger than any of its parts.

Chapter 4 Exercise

Landau suggests that the Constitution established a "self-regulating" system. Explain what Landau means by self-regulating system and how such a concept can be helpful in understanding the structure of our government.

Landau observed that the Constitution provides for a flat organization structure. What is a flat organization structure and what does it suggest about decision-making, efficiency, and responsibility within our political system?

CHAPTER 5

Federalism

Merits of the Federal System

James Bryce

James Bryce analyzes the basis and merits of American Federalism. He notes the inherent flexibility and adaptability of federalism and underscores the importance of balance between states and federal governments.

There are two distinct lines of argument by which their federal system was recommended to the framers of the Constitution, and upon which it is still held forth for imitation to other countries. These lines have been so generally confounded that it is well to present them in a precise form.

The first set of arguments point to federalism proper, and are the following:

1. That federalism furnishes the means of uniting commonwealths into one nation under one national government without extinguishing their separate administrations, legislatures, and local patriotisms. As the Americans of 1787 would probably have preferred complete state independence to the fusion of their states into a unified government, federalism was the only resource. So when the new Germanic Empire, which is really a federation, was established in 1871, Bavaria and Würtemberg could not have been brought under a national government save by a federal scheme.

Similar suggestions, as everyone knows, have been made for resettling the relations of Ireland to Great Britain, and of the self-governing British colonies to the United Kingdom. There are causes and conditions which dispose nations living under loosely compacted governments, to form a closer union in a federal form. There are other causes and conditions which dispose the subjects of one government, or sections of these subjects, to desire to make their governmental union less close by substituting a federal for a unitary system. In both sets of cases, the centripetal or centrifugal forces spring from the local position, the history, the sentiments, the economic needs of those among whom the problem arises; and that which is good for one people or political body is not necessarily good for another. Federalism is an equally legitimate resource where it is adopted for the sake of tightening or for the sake of loosening a preexisting bond.[1]

1. I have treated of this subject in an essay on the centripetal and centrifugal forces in constitutional law in a book entitled *Studies in History and Jurisprudence*.

2. That federalism supplies the best means of developing a new and vast country. It permits an expansion whose extent, and whose rate and manner of progress, cannot be foreseen to proceed with more variety of methods, more adaptation of laws and administration to the circumstances of each part of the territory, and altogether in a more truly natural and spontaneous way, than can be expected under a centralized government, which is disposed to apply its settled system through all its dominions. Thus the special needs of a new region are met by the inhabitants in the way they find best: its laws can be adapted to the economic conditions which from time to time present themselves; its special evils are cured by special remedies, perhaps more drastic than an old country demands, perhaps more lax than an old country would tolerate; while at the same time the spirit of self-reliance among those who build up these new communities is stimulated and respected.

3. That federalism prevents the rise of a despotic central government, absorbing other powers, and menacing the private liberties of the citizen. This may now seem to have been an idle fear, so far as America was concerned. It was however, a very real fear among the ancestors of the present Americans, and nearly led to the rejection even of so undespotic an instrument as the federal Constitution of 1789. Congress (or the president, as the case may be) is still sometimes described as a tyrant by the party which does not control it, simply because it is a central government; and the states are represented as bulwarks against its encroachments.

The second set of arguments relate to and recommend not so much federalism as local self-government. I state them briefly because they are familiar.

4. Self-government stimulates the interest of people in the affairs of their neighbourhood, sustains local political life, educates the citizen in his daily rund of civic duty, teaches him that perpetual vigilance and the sacrifice of his own time and labour are the price that must be paid for individual liberty and collective prosperity.

5. Self-government secures the good administration of local affairs by giving the inhabitants of each locality due means of overseeing the conduct of their business.

That these two sets of grounds are distinct appears from the fact that the sort of local interest which local self-government evokes is quite a different thing from the interest men feel in the affairs of a large body like an American state. So, too, the control over its own affairs of a township, or even a small county, where everybody can know what is going on, is quite different from the control exercisable over the affairs of a commonwealth with a million of people. Local self-government may exist in a unified country like England, and may be wanting in a federal country like Germany. And in America itself, while some states, like those of New England possessed an admirably complete system of local government, others, such as Virginia, the old champion of state sovereignty, were imperfectly provided with it. Nevertheless, through both sets of arguments there runs the general principle, applicable in every part and branch of government, that, where other things are equal, the more power is given to the units which compose the nation, be they large or small, and the less to the nation as a whole and to its central authority, so much the fuller will be the liberties and so much greater the energy of the individuals who compose the people. This principle, though it had not been then formulated in the way men formulate it now, was heartily embraced by the Americans. Perhaps it was because they agreed in taking it as an axiom that they seldom referred to it in the subsequent controversies regarding state rights. These controversies proceeded on the basis of the Constitution as a law rather than on considerations of general political theory. A European reader of the history of the first seventy years of the United States is surprised how little is said, through the interminable discussions regarding the relation of the federal government to the states, on the respective advantages of centralization or localization of powers as a matter of historical experience and general expediency.

Three further benefits to be expected from a federal system may be mentioned, benefits which seem to have been unnoticed or little regarded by those who established it in America.

6. Federalism enables a people to try experiments in legislation and administration which could not be safely tried in a large centralized country. A comparatively small commonwealth like an American state easily makes and unmakes its laws; mistakes are not serious, for they are soon corrected; other states profit by the experience of a law or a method which has worked well or ill in the state that has tried it.

7. Federalism, if it diminishes the collective force of a nation, diminishes also the risks to which its size and the diversities of its parts expose it. A nation so divided is like a ship built with watertight compartments. When a leak is sprung in one compartment, the cargo stowed there may be damaged, but the other compartments remain dry and keep the ship afloat. So if social discord or an economic crisis has produced disorders or foolish legislation in one member of the federal body, the mischief may stop at the state frontier instead of spreading through and tainting the nation at large.

8. Federalism, by creating many local legislatures with wide powers, relieves the national legislature of a part of that large mass of functions which might otherwise prove too heavy for it. Thus business is more promptly despatched, and the great central council of the nation has time to deliberate on those questions which most nearly touch the whole country.

All of these arguments recommending federalism have proved valid in American experience.

The problem which all federalized nations have to solve is how to secure an efficient central government and preserve national unity, while allowing free scope for the diversities, and free play to the authorities, of the members of the federation. It is to adopt that favourite astronomical metaphor which no American panegyrist of the Constitution omits, to keep the centrifugal and centripetal forces in equilibrium, so that neither the planet states shall fly off into space, nor the sun of the central government draw them into its consuming fires. The characteristic merit of the American Constitution lies in the method by which it has solved this problem. It has given the national government a direct authority over all citizens, irrespective of the state governments, and has therefore been able safely to leave wide powers in the hands of those governments. And by placing the Constitution above both the national and the state governments, it has referred the arbitrament of disputes between them to an independent body, charged with the interpretation of the Constitution, a body which is to be deemed not so much a third authority in the government as the living voice of the Constitution, the unfolder of the mind of the people whose will stands expressed in that supreme instrument.

The application of these two principles, unknown to or at any rate little used by, any previous federation,[2] has contributed more than anything else to the stability of the American system, and to the reverence which its citizens feel for it, a reverence which is the best security for its permanence, Yet even these devices would not have succeeded but for the presence of mass of moral and material influences stronger than any political devices, which have maintained the equilibrium of centrifugal and centripetal forces. On the one hand there has been the love of local independence and self-government; on the other, the sense of community in blood, in language, in habits and ideas, a common pride in the national history and the national flag.

---

2. The central government in the Achæan League had apparently a direct authority over the citizens of the several cities, but it was so ill defined and so little employed that we can hardly cite that instance as a precedent.

Chapter 5 Exercise

Bryce listed several benefits of federalism. Identify and discuss two such benefits.

What problem must federalism solve in our political system? Explain your answer.

PART IV

Civil Liberties and Civil Rights

CHAPTER 6

Limiting Speech

A Clear and Present Danger
Schenck vs. United States

Justice Oliver Wendell Holmes

Justice Oliver Wendell Holmes provides the opinion in *Schenck v. United States* (1919). Most notably, Holmes observed that constitutional rights (here, first amendment) are limited and circumscribed by political circumstances.

Holmes, J. This is an indictment in three counts. The first charges a conspiracy to violate the Espionage Act of June 15, 1917 . . . by causing and attempting to cause insubordination, &c., in the military and naval forces of the United States, and to obstruct the recruiting and enlistment service of the United States, when the United States was at war with the German Empire, to wit, that the defendants wilfully conspired to have printed and circulated to men who had been called and accepted for military service under the Act of May 18, 1917, a document set forth and alleged to be calculated to cause such insubordination and obstruction. The count alleges over acts in pursuance of the conspiracy, ending in the distribution of the document set forth. . . . They set up the First Amendment to the Constitution forbidding Congress to make any law abridging the freedom of speech, or of the press, and bring-

ing the case here on that ground have argued some other points also of which we must dispose.

It is argued that the evidence, if admissible, was not sufficient to prove that the defendant Schenck was concerned in sending the documents. According to the testimony Schenck said he was general secretary of the Socialist party and had charge of the Socialist headquarters from which the documents were sent. He identified a book found there as the minutes of the Executive Committee of the party. The book showed a resolution of August 13, 1917, that 15,000 leaflets should be printed on the other side of one of them in use, to be mailed to men who had passed exemption boards, and for distribution. Schenck personally tended to the printing. On August 20 the general secretary's report said, "Obtained new leaflets from printer and started work addressing envelopes" &c.; and there was a resolve that Comrade Schenck be allowed $125 for sending leaflets through the mail. He said that he had about fifteen or sixteen thousand printed. There were files of the circular in question in the inner office which he said were printed on the other side of the one sided circular and were there for distribution. Other copies were proved to have been sent through the mails to drafted men. Without going into confirmatory details that were proved, no reasonable man could doubt that the defendant Schenck was largely instrumental in sending the circulars about. . . .

The document in question upon its first printed side recited the first section of the Thirteenth Amendment, said that the idea embodied in it was violated by the Conscription Act and that a conscript is little better than a convict. In impassioned language it intimated that conscription was despotism in its worse form and a monstrous wrong against humanity in the interest of Wall Street's chosen few. It said, "Do not submit to intimidation," but in form at least confined itself to peaceful measures such as a petition for the repeal of the act. The other and later printed side of the sheet was headed "Assert Your Rights." It stated reasons for alleging that any one violated the Constitution when he refused to recognize "your right to assert your opposition to the draft," and went on "If you do not assert and support your rights, you are helping to deny or disparage rights which it is the solemn duty of all citizens and residents of the United States to retain." It described the arguments on the other side as coming from cunning politicians and a mercenary capitalist press, and even silent consent to the conscription law as helping to support an infamous conspiracy. It denied the power to send our citizens away to foreign shores to shoot up the people of other lands, and added that words could not express the condemnation such cold-blooded ruthlessness deserves, &c., &c., winding up "You must do your share to maintain, support and uphold the rights of the people of this country." Of course the document would not have been sent unless it had been intended to have some effect, and we do not see what effect it could be expected to have upon persons subject to the draft except to influence them to obstruct the carrying of it out. The defendants do not deny that the jury might find against them on this point.

But it is said, suppose that that was the tendency of this circular, it is protected by the First Amendment to the Constitution. . . . We admit that in many places and in ordinary times the defendants in saying all that was said in the circular would have been within their constitutional rights. But the character of every act depends upon the circumstances in which it is done. The most stringent protection of free speech would not protect a man in falsely shouting fire in a theater and causing a panic. It does not even protect a man from an injunction against uttering words that may have all the effect of force. The question in every case is whether the words used are used in such circumstances and are of such a nature as to create a clear and present danger that they will bring about the substantive evils that Congress has a right to prevent. It is a question of proximity and degree. When a nation is at war many things that might be said in time of peace are such a hindrance to its effort that their utterance will not be endured so long as men fight and that no Court could regard them as protected by any constitutional right. It seems to be admitted that if an actual obstruction of the recruiting service were proved, liability for words that produced that effect might be enforced. The statute of 1917 in sec. 4 punishes conspiracies to obstruct as well as actual obstruction. If the act, (speaking, or circulating a paper,) its tendency and the intent with which it is done are the same, we perceive no ground for saying that success alone warrants making the act a crime. . . .

Judgments affirmed.

—Justice Oliver Wendell Holmes, Opinion in Schenck *v.* United States, 1919

Chapter 6 Exercise

Does Congress have a right to limit our first amendment rights? Outline the logic provided by Holmes.

CHAPTER 7

Freeing Speechmakers

The Indispensable Opposition

Walter Lippman

Walter Lippmann argues that freedom of speech is not simply an individual right of expression. Rather, free speech serves two important functions in our democracy: (1) others' right to free speech improves our own opinions; (2) right to speech is indispensable because it acts as a process for finding the truth.

Were they pressed hard enough, most men would probably confess that political freedom—that is to say, the right to speak freely and to act in opposition—is a noble ideal rather than a practical necessity. As the case for freedom is generally put today, the argument lends itself to this feeling. It is made to appear that, whereas each man claims his freedom as a matter of right, the freedom he accords to other men is a matter of toleration. Thus, the defense of freedom of opinion tends to rest not on its substantial, beneficial, and indispensable consequences, but on a somewhat eccentric, a rather vaguely benevolent, attachment to an abstraction.

It is all very well to say with Voltaire, "I wholly disapprove of what you say, but will defend to the death your right to say it," but as a matter of fact most men will not defend to the death the rights of other men: if they disapprove sufficiently what other men say, they will somehow suppress those men if they can.

So, if this is the best that can be said for liberty of opinion, that a man must tolerate his opponents because every one has a "right" to say what he pleases, then we shall find that liberty of opinion is a luxury, safe only in pleasant times when men can be tolerant because they are not deeply and vitally concerned.

Yet actually, as a matter of historic fact, there is a much stronger foundation for the great constitutional right of freedom of speech, and as a matter of practical human experience there is a much more compelling reason for cultivating the habits of free men. We take, it seems to me, a naïvely self-righteous view when we argue as if the right of our opponents to speak were something that we protect because we are magnanimous, noble, and unselfish. The compelling reason why, if liberty of opinion did not exist, we should have to invent it, why it will eventually have to be restored in all civilized countries where it is now suppressed, is that we must protect the right of our opponents to speak because we must hear what they have to say.

We miss the whole point when we imagine that we tolerate the freedom of our political opponents as we tolerate a howling baby next door, as we put up with the blasts from our neighbor's radio because we are too peaceable to heave a brick through the window. If this were all there is to freedom of opinion, that we are too good-natured or too timid to anything about our opponents and our critics except to let them talk, it would be difficult to say whether we are tolerant because we are magnanimous or because we are lazy, because we have strong principles or because we lack serious convictions, whether we have the hospitality of an inquiring mind or the indifference of an empty mind. And so, if we truly wish to understand why freedom is necessary in a civilized society, we must begin by realizing that, because freedom of discussion improves our own opinions, the liberties of other men are our own vital necessity.

We are much closer to the essence of the matter, not when we quote Voltaire, but when we go to the doctor and pay him to ask us the most embarrassing questions and to prescribe the most disagreeable diet. When we pay the doctor to exercise complete freedom of speech about the cause and cure of our stomachache, we do not look upon ourselves as tolerant and magnanimous, and worthy to be admired by ourselves. We have enough common sense to know that if we threaten to put the doctor in jail because we do not like the diagnosis and the prescription it will be unpleasant for the doctor, to be sure, but equally unpleasant for our own stomachache. That is why even the most ferocious dictator would rather be treated by a doctor who was free

to think and speak the truth than by his own Minister of Propaganda. For there is a point, the point at which things really matter, where the freedom of others is no longer a question of their right but of our own need.

The point at which we recognize this need is much higher in some men than in others. The totalitarian rulers think they do not need the freedom of an opposition: they exile, imprison, or shoot their opponents. We have concluded on the basis of practical experience, which goes back to Magna Carta and beyond, that we need the opposition. We pay the opposition salaries out of the public treasury.

In so far as the usual apology for freedom of speech ignores this experience, it becomes abstract and eccentric rather than concrete and human. The emphasis is generally put on the right to speak, as if all that mattered were that the doctor should be free to go out into the park and explain to the vacant air why I have a stomachache. Surely that is a miserable caricature of the great civic right which men have bled and died for. What really matters is that the doctor should tell *me* what ails me, that I should listen to him; that if I do not like what he says I should be free to call in another doctor; and that then the first doctor should have to listen to the second doctor; and that out of all the speaking and listening, the give-and-take of opinions, the truth should be arrived at.

This is the creative principle of freedom of speech, not that it is a system for the tolerating of error, but that it is a system for finding the truth. It may not produce the truth, or the whole truth all the time, or often, or in some cases ever. But if the truth can be found, there is no other system which will normally and habitually find so much truth. Until we have thoroughly understood this principle, we shall not know why we must value our liberty, or how we can protect and develop it. . . .

The only reason for dwelling on all this is that if we are to preserve democracy we must understand its principles. And the principle which distinguishes it from all other forms of government is that in a democracy the opposition not only is tolerated as constitutional but must be maintained because it is in fact indispensable.

The democratic system cannot be operated without effective opposition. For, in making the great experiment of governing people by consent rather than by coercion, it is not sufficient that the party in power should have a majority. It is just as necessary that the party in power should never outrage the minority. That means that it must listen to the minority and be moved by the criticisms of the minority. That means that its measures must take account of the minority's objections, and that in administering measures it must remember that the minority may become the majority.

The opposition is indispensable. A good statesman, like any other sensible human being, always learns more from his opponents than from his fervent supporters. For his supporters will push him to disaster unless his opponents show him where the dangers are. So if he is wise, he will often pray to be delivered from his friends, because they will ruin him. But, though it hurts, he ought also to pray never to be left without opponents; for they keep him on the path of reason and good sense.

The national unity of a free people depends upon a sufficiently even balance of political power to make it impracticable for the administration to be arbitrary and for the opposition to be revolutionary and irreconcilable. Where that balance no longer exists, democracy perishes. For unless all the citizens of a state are forced by circumstances to compromise, unless they feel that they can affect policy but that no one can wholly dominate it, unless by habit and necessity they have to give and take, freedom cannot be maintained.

Name: _____ Date: _____

Chapter 7 Exercise

Discuss the connection between free speech and truth.

Why does Lippmann believe political opposition is indispensable to our political system?

Chapter 8

Separate but Equal

Plessy v. Ferguson Mandate

Jean West Mueller and Wynell Burroughs Schamel

Jean Mueller and Wynell Schamel outline the political circumstances that preceded the famous *Plessy v. Ferguson* case. Of interest is the strategy of African Americans in Louisiana, the local, state, and federal responses to constitutional amendments during Reconstruction, and the Supreme Court interpretation of the 14th amendment. Importantly, such events were prologue for *Brown v. Board of Education*.

During the era of Reconstruction, black Americans' political rights were affirmed by three constitutional amendments and numerous laws passed by Congress. Racial discrimination was attacked on a particularly broad front by the Civil Rights Act of 1875. This legislation made it a crime for an individual to deny "the full and equal enjoyment of any of the accommodations, advantages, facilities, and privileges of inns, public conveyances on land or water, theaters and other places of public amusement; subject only to the conditions and limitations established by law, and applicable alike to citizens of every race and color."

In 1883, the Supreme Court struck down the 1875 act, ruling that the Fourteenth Amendment did not give Congress authority to prevent discrimination by private individuals. Victims of racial discrimination were told to seek relief not from the federal government, but from the states. Unfortunately, state governments were passing legislation that codified inequality between the races. Laws requiring the establishment of separate schools for children of each race were most common; however, segregation was soon extended to encompass most public and semipublic facilities.

Beginning with passage of an 1887 Florida law, states began to require that railroads furnish

"Plessy v. Ferguson Mandate," by Jean West Mueller and Wynell Burroughs Schamel, *Social Education,* 53, no. 2 (1989): 120–122. © 1989 National Council for the Social Studies. Reprinted by permission.

separate accommodations for each race. These measures were unpopular with the railway companies that bore the expense of adding Jim Crow cars. Segregation of the railroads was even more objectionable to black citizens who saw it as a further step toward the total repudiation of three constitutional amendments. When such a bill was proposed before the Louisiana legislature in 1890, the articulate black community of New Orleans protested vigorously. Nonetheless, despite the presence of 16 black legislators in the state assembly, the law was passed. It required either separate passenger coaches or partitioned coaches to provide segregated accommodations for each race. Passengers were required to sit in the appropriate areas or face a $25 fine or a 20-day jail sentence. Black nurses attending white children were permitted to ride in white compartments, however.

In 1891, a group of concerned young black men of New Orleans formed the "Citizens' Committee to Test the Constitutionality of the Separate Car Law." They raised money and engaged Albion W. Tourgée, a prominent Radical Republican author and politician, as their lawyer. On May 15, 1892, the Louisiana State Supreme Court decided in favor of the Pullman Company's claim that the law was unconstitutional as it applied to interstate travel. Encouraged, the committee decided to press a test case on intrastate travel. With the cooperation of the East Louisiana Railroad, on June 7, 1892, Homer Plessy, a mulatto (7/8 white), seated himself in a white compartment, was challenged by the conductor, and was arrested and charged with violating the state law. In the Criminal District court for the Parish of Orleans, Tourgée argued that the law requiring "separate but equal accommodations" was unconstitutional. When Judge John H. Ferguson ruled against him, Plessy applied to the State Supreme Court for a writ of prohibition and certiorari. Although the court upheld the state law, it granted Plessy's petition for a writ of error that would enable him to appeal the case to the Supreme Court.

In 1896, the Supreme Court issued its decision in *Plessy v. Ferguson*. Justice Henry Brown of Michigan delivered the majority opinion, which sustained the constitutionality of Louisiana's Jim Crow law. In part, he said:

> We consider the underlying fallacy of the plaintiff's argument to consist in the assumption that the enforced separation of the two races stamps the colored race with a badge of inferiority. If this be so, it is not by reason of anything found in the act, but solely because the colored race chooses to put that construction upon it. . . . The argument also assumes that social prejudices may be overcome by legislation, and that equal rights cannot be secured except by an enforced commingling of the two races. . . . If the civil and political rights of both races be equal, one cannot be inferior to the other civilly or politically. If one race be inferior to the other socially, the Constitution of the United States cannot put them upon the same plane.

In a powerful dissent, conservative Kentuckian John Marshall Harlan wrote:

> I am of the opinion that the statute of Louisiana is inconsistent with the personal liberty of citizens, white and black, in the State, and hostile to both the spirit and the letter of the Constitution of the United States. If laws of like character should be enacted in the several States of the Union, the effect would be in the highest degree mischievous. Slavery as an institution tolerated by law would, it is true, have disappeared from our country, but there would remain a power in the States, by sinister legislation, to interfere with the blessings of freedom; to regulate civil rights common to all citizens, upon the basis of race; and to place in a condition of legal inferiority a large body of American citizens, now constituting a part of the political community, called the people of the United States, for whom and by whom, through representatives, our government is administered. Such a system is inconsistent with the guarantee given by the Constitution to each State of a republican form of government, and may be stricken down by congressional action, or by the courts in the discharge of their solemn duty to maintain the supreme law of the land, anything in the Constitution or laws of any State to the contrary notwithstanding.

Indeed, it was through the Supreme Court's decision in *Brown v. Board of Education of Topeka, Kansas* and congressional civil rights acts of the 1950s and 1960s that systemic segregation under state law was ended. In the wake of those federal actions, many states amended or rewrote their state constitutions to conform with the spirit of the Fourteenth Amendment. But for Homer Plessy the remedies came too late. . . .

Chapter 8 Exercise

Identify and discuss the key events that led to the *Plessy v. Ferguson* case.

Why were the three constitutional amendments passed during Reconstruction so ineffective against discrimination?

PART V

Congress

CHAPTER 9

Electoral Incentive

Congress: The Electoral Connection

David Mayhew

Congressional scholar David Mayhew asserts that to understand Congress and its members we must recognize the importance of the electoral connection. The primary motivator of congressional behavior is reelection. Accordingly, congressional members constantly engage in activities that enhance their reelection chances.

. . . I shall conjure up a vision of United States congressmen as single-minded seekers of reelection, see what kinds of activity that goal implies, and then speculate about how congressmen so motivated are likely to go about building and sustaining legislative institutions and making policy. . . .

I find an emphasis on the reelection goal attractive for a number of reasons. First, I think it fits political reality rather well. Second, it puts the spotlight directly on men rather than on parties and pressure groups, which in the past have often entered discussions of American politics as analytic phantoms. Third, I think politics is best studied as a struggle among men to gain and maintain power and the consequences of that struggle. Fourth—and perhaps most important—the

reelection quest establishes an accountability relationship with an electorate, and any serious thinking about democratic theory has to give a central place to the question of accountability. . . .

Whether they are safe or marginal, cautious or audacious, congressmen must constantly engage in activities related to reelection. There will be differences in emphasis, but all members share the root need to do things—indeed, to do things day in and day out during their terms. The next step here is to present a typology, a short list of the *kinds* of activities congressmen find it electorally useful to engage in. . . .

One activity is *advertising*, defined here as any effort to disseminate one's name among constituents in such a fashion as to create a favorable image but in messages having little or no issue content. A successful congressman builds what amounts to a brand name, which may have a generalized electoral value for other politicians in the same family. The personal qualities to emphasize are experience, knowledge, responsiveness, concern, sincerity, independence, and the like. Just getting one's name across is difficult enough; only about half the electorate, if asked, can supply their House members' names. It helps a congressman to be known. "In the main, recognition carries a positive valence; to be perceived at all is to be perceived favorably." A vital advantage enjoyed by House incumbents is that they are much better known among voters than their November challengers. They are better known because they spend a great deal of time, energy, and money trying to make themselves better known. There are standard routines—frequent visits to the constituency, nonpolitical speeches to home audiences, the sending out of infant care booklets and letters of condolence and congratulation. . . .

Some routines are less standard. Congressman George E. Shipley (D., Ill.) claims to have met personally about half his constituents (i.e. some 200,000 people). For over twenty years Congressman Charles C. Diggs, Jr. (D., Mich.) has run a radio program featuring himself as a "combination disc jockey—commentator and minister." Congressman Daniel J. Flood (D., Pa.) is "famous for appearing unannounced and often uninvited at wedding anniversaries and other events." Anniversaries and other events aside, congressional advertising is done largely at public expense. Use of the franking privilege has mushroomed in recent years; in early 1973 one estimate predicted that House and Senate members would send out about 476 million pieces of mail in the year 1974, at a public cost of $38.1 million—or about 900,000 pieces per member with a subsidy of $70,000 per member. By far the heaviest mailroom traffic comes in Octobers of even-numbered years. There are some differences between House and Senate members in the ways they go about getting their names across. House members are free to blanket their constituencies with mailings for all boxholders; sen-

ators are not. But senators find it easier to appear on national television—for example, in short reaction statements on the nightly news shows. Advertising is a staple congressional activity, and there is no end to it. For each member there are always new voters to be apprised of his worthiness and old voters to be reminded of it.

A second activity may be called *credit claiming, defined here as acting so as to generate a belief* in a relevant political actor (or actors) that one is personally responsible for causing the government, or some unit thereof, to do something that the actor (or actors) considers desirable. The political logic of this, from the congressman's point of view, is that an actor who believes that a member can make pleasing things happen will no doubt wish to keep him in office so that he can make pleasing things happen in the future. The emphasis here is on individual accomplishment (rather than, say, party or governmental accomplishment) and on the congressman as doer (rather than as, say, expounder of constituency views). Credit claiming is highly important to congressmen, with the consequence that much of congressional life is a relentless search for opportunities to engage in it.

Where can credit be found? . . . For the average congressman the staple way of doing this is to traffic in what may be called "particularized benefits." . . .

In sheer volume the bulk of particularized benefits come under the heading of "casework"—the thousands of favors congressional offices perform for supplicants in ways that normally do not require legislative action. High school students ask for essay materials, soldiers for emergency leaves, pensioners for location of missing checks, local governments for grant information, and on and on. Each office has skilled professionals who can play the bureaucracy like an organ—pushing the right pedals to produce the desired effects. But many benefits require new legislation, or at least they require important allocative decisions on matters covered by existent legislation. Here the congressman fills the traditional role of supplier of goods to the home district. It is a believable role; when a member claims credit for a benefit on the order of a dam, he may well receive it. Shiny construction projects seem especially useful. . . .

The third activity congressmen engage in may be called *position taking*, defined here as the public enunciation of a judgmental statement on anything likely to be of interest to political actors. The statement may take the form of a roll call vote. The most important classes of judgmental statements are those prescribing American governmental ends (a vote cast against the war; a statement that "the war should be ended immediately") or governmental means (a statement that "the way to end the war is to take it to the United Nations"). . . .

The ways in which positions can be registered are numerous and often imaginative. There are floor addresses ranging from weighty orations to mass-produced "nationality day statements." There are speeches before home groups, television appearances, letters, newsletters, press releases, ghostwritten books, *Playboy* articles, even interviews with political scientists. . . . Outside the roll call process the congressman is usually able to tailor his positions to suit his audiences. . . .

. . . On a controversial issue a Capitol Hill office normally prepares two form letters to send out to constituent letter writers—one for the pros and one (not directly contradictory) for the antis. Handling discrete audiences in person requires simple agility, a talent well demonstrated in this selection from a Nader profile:

> "You may find this difficult to understand," said Democrat Edward R. Roybal, the Mexican-American representative from California's thirtieth district, "but sometimes I wind up making a patriotic speech one afternoon and later on that same day an anti-war speech. In the patriotic speech I speak of past wars but I also speak of the need to prevent more wars. My positions are not inconsistent; I just approach different people differently." Roybal went on to depict the diversity of crowds he speaks to: one afternoon he is surrounded by balding men wearing Veterans' caps and holding American flags; a few hours later he speaks to a crowd of Chicano youths, angry over American involvement in Vietnam. Such a diverse constituency, Roybal believes, calls for different methods of expressing one's convictions.

Indeed it does.

Chapter 9 Exercise

Identify and discuss potential biases in representation that may result from the constant drive for reelection.

Describe and illustrate with examples three strategies that congressional members engage in to attain reelection.

PART VI

Presidency

CHAPTER 10

Paradox

The Paradoxes of the American Presidency

Thomas Cronin and Michael Genovese

The Presidency is an office of paradoxes. Thomas Cronin and Michael Genovese identify nine paradoxes and use them to illustrate the diverse expectations citizens hold of their presidents. For example, Cronin and Genovese observe that we demand "powerful, popular presidential leadership that solves the nation's problems but also we are inherently suspicious of strong controlled leadership...therefore we place significant limits on presidential power." Given such expectations, it is not difficult to appreciate the often inconsistent, contradictory behavior of our presidents.

The mind searches for answers to the complexities of life. We often gravitate toward simple explanations for the world's mysteries. This is a natural way to try and make sense out of a world that seems to defy understanding. We are uncomfortable with contradictions so we reduce reality to understandable simplifications. And yet, contradictions and clashing expectations are part of life. "No aspect of society, no habit, custom, movement, development, is without crosscurrents," says historian Barbara Tuchman. "Starving peasants in hovels live alongside prosperous landlords in featherbeds. Children are neglected and children are loved." In life we are confronted with paradoxes for which we seek meaning. The same is true for the American presidency. We admire presidential power, yet fear it. We yearn for the heroic, yet are also inherently suspicious of it. We demand dynamic leadership, yet grant only limited powers to the president. We want presidents to be dispassionate analysts and listeners, yet they must also be decisive. We are impressed with presidents who have great self-confidence, yet we dislike arrogance and respect those who express reasonable self-doubt.

How then are we to make sense of the presidency? This complex, multidimensional, even contradictory institution is vital to the American system of government. The physical and political laws that seem to constrain one president, liberate another. What proves successful in one, leads to failure in another. Rather than seeking one unifying theory of presidential politics that answers all our questions, we believe that the American presidency might be better understood as a series of paradoxes, clashing expectations and contradictions.

Leaders live with contradictions. Presidents, more than most people, learn to take advantage of contrary or divergent forces. Leadership situations commonly require successive displays of contrasting characteristics. Living with, even embracing, contradictions is a sign of political and personal maturity.

The effective leader understands the presence of opposites. The aware leader, much like a first-rate conductor, knows when to bring in various sections, knows when and how to turn the volume up and down, and learns how to balance opposing sections to achieve desired results. Effective presidents learn how to manage these contradictions and give meaning and purpose to confusing and often clashing expectations. The novelist F. Scott Fitzgerald once suggested that, "The test of a first-rate intelligence is the ability to hold two opposed ideas in the mind at the same time." Casey Stengel, long-time New York Yankee manager and occasional (if accidental) Zen philosopher, captured the essence of the paradox when he noted, "Good pitching will always stop good hitting, and vice versa."

Our expectations of, and demands on, the president are frequently so contradictory as to invite two-faced behavior by our presidents. Presidential powers are often not as great as many of us believe, and the president gets unjustly condemned as ineffective. Or a president will overreach or resort to unfair play while trying to live up to our demands.

The Constitution is of little help. The founders purposely left the presidency imprecisely defined. This was due in part to their fears of both the monarchy and the masses, and in part to their hopes that future presidents would create a more powerful office than the framers were able to do at the time. They knew that at times the president would have to move swiftly and effec-

tively, yet they went to considerable lengths to avoid enumerating specific powers and duties in order to calm the then widespread fear of monarchy. After all, the nation had just fought a war against executive tyranny. Thus the paradox of the invention of the presidency: To get the presidency approved in 1787 and 1788, the framers had to leave several silences and ambiguities for fear of portraying the office as an overly centralized leadership institution. Yet when we need central leadership we turn to the president and read into Article II of the Constitution various prerogatives or inherent powers that allow the president to perform as an effective national leader.

Today the informal and symbolic powers of the presidency account for as much as the formal, stated ones. Presidential powers expand and contract in response to varying situational and technological changes. The powers of the presidency are thus interpreted so differently that they sometimes seem to be those of different offices. In some ways the modern presidency has virtually unlimited authority for almost anything its occupant chooses to do with it. In other ways, a president seems hopelessly ensnarled in a web of checks and balances.

Presidents and presidential candidates must constantly balance conflicting demands, cross pressures, and contradictions. It is characteristic of the American mind to hold contradictory ideas without bothering to resolve the conflicts between them. Perhaps some contradictions are best left unresolved, especially as ours is an imperfect world and our political system is a complicated one, held together by countless compromises. We may not be able to resolve many of these clashing expectations. Some of the inconsistencies in our judgments about presidents doubtless stem from the many ironies and paradoxes of the human condition. While difficult, at the least we should develop a better understanding of what it is we ask of our presidents, thereby increasing our sensitivity to the limits and possibilities of what a president can achieve. This might free presidents to lead and administer more effectively in those critical times when the nation has no choice but to turn to them. Whether we like it or not, the vitality of our democracy depends in large measure upon the sensitive interaction of presidential leadership with an understanding public willing to listen and willing to provide support. Carefully planned innovation is nearly impossible without the kind of leadership a competent and fair-minded president can provide.

The following are some of the paradoxes of the presidency. Some are cases of confused expectations. Some are cases of wanting one kind of presidential behavior at one time, and another kind later. Still others stem from the contradiction inherent in the concept of democratic leadership, which on the surface at least, appears to set up "democratic" and "leadership" as warring concepts. Whatever the source, each has implications for presidential performance and for how Americans judge presidential success and failure. . . .

Paradox #1. Americans demand powerful, popular presidential leadership that solves the nation's problems. Yet we are inherently suspicious of strong centralized leadership and especially the abuse of power and therefore we place significant limits on the president's powers.

We admire power but fear it. We love to unload responsibilities on our leaders, yet we intensely dislike being bossed around. We expect impressive leadership from presidents, and we simultaneously impose constitutional, cultural, and political restrictions on them. These restrictions often prevent presidents from living up to our expectations. . . .

Presidents are supposed to follow the laws and respect the constitutional procedures that were designed to restrict their power, yet still they must be powerful and effective when action is needed. For example, we approve of presidential military initiatives and covert operations when they work out well, but we criticize presidents and insist they work more closely with Congress when the initiatives fail. We recognize the need for secrecy in certain government actions, but we resent being deceived and left in the dark—again, especially when things go wrong, as in Reagan's Iranian arms sale diversions to the Contras.

Although we sometimes do not approve of the way a president acts, we often approve of the end results. Thus Lincoln is often criticized for acting outside the limits of the Constitution, but at the same time he is forgiven due to the obvious necessity for him to violate certain constitutional principles in order to preserve the Union. FDR was often flagrantly deceptive and manipulative not only of his political opponents but also of his staff and allies. FDR even relished pushing people around and toying with them. But leadership effectiveness in the end often comes down to whether a person acts in terms of the highest interests of the nation. Most historians conclude Lincoln and Roosevelt were responsible in the use of presidential power, to preserve the Union, to fight the depression and nazism. Historians also conclude that Nixon was wrong for acting beyond the law in pursuit of personal power. . . .

Paradox #2. We yearn for the democratic "common person" and also for the uncommon, charismatic, heroic, visionary performance.

We want our presidents to be like us, but better than us. We like to think America is the land where the common sense of the common person reigns. Nourished on a diet of Frank Capra's "common-man-as-hero" movies, and the literary celebration of the average citizen by authors such as Emerson, Whitman, and Thoreau, we prize the common touch. The plain-speaking Harry Truman, the up-from-the-log-cabin "man or woman of the people," is enticing. Few of us, however, settle for anything but the best; we want presidents to succeed and we hunger for brilliant, uncommon, and semiregal performances from presidents. . . .

It is said the American people crave to be governed by a president who is greater than anyone else yet not better than themselves. We are inconsistent; we want our president to be one of the folks yet also something special. If presidents get too special, however, they get criticized and roasted. If they try to be too folksy, people get bored. We cherish the myth that anyone can grow up to be president, that there are no barriers and no elite qualifications, but we don't want someone who too ordinary. Would-be presidents have to prove their special qualifications—their excellence, their stamina, and their capacity for uncommon leadership. Fellow commoner, Truman, rose to the demands of the job and became an apparently gifted decision maker, or so his admirers would have us believe.

In 1976 Governor Jimmy Carter seemed to grasp this conflict and he ran as local, down-home, farm-boy-next-door makes good. The image of the peanut farmer turned gifted governor contributed greatly to Carter's success as a national candidate and he used it with consummate skill. Early in his presidential bid, Carter enjoyed introducing himself as peanut farmer *and* nuclear physicist, once again suggesting he was down to earth but cerebral as well.

Ronald Reagan illustrated another aspect of this paradox. He was a representative all-American—small-town, midwestern, and also a rich celebrity of stage, screen, and television. He boasted of having been a Democrat, yet campaigned as a Republican. A veritable Mr. Smith goes to Washington, he also had uncommon star quality. Bill Clinton liked us to view him as both a Rhodes scholar and an ordinary saxophone-playing member of the high school band from Hope, Arkansas; as a John Kennedy and even an Elvis figure; and also as just another jogger who would stop by for a Big Mac on the way home from a run in the neighborhood. . . .

Paradox #3. We want a decent, just, caring, and compassionate president, yet we admire a cunning, guileful, and, on occasions that warrant it, even a ruthless, manipulative president.

There is always a fine line between boldness and recklessness, between strong self-confidence and what the Greeks called "hubris," between dogged determination and pigheaded stubbornness. Opinion polls indicate people want a just, decent, and intellectually honest individual as our chief executive. Almost as strongly, however, the public also demands the quality of toughness.

We may admire modesty, humility, and a sense of proportion, but most of our great leaders have been vain and crafty. After all, you don't get to the White House by being a wallflower. Most have aggressively sought power and were rarely preoccupied with metaphysical inquiry or ethical considerations.

Franklin Roosevelt's biographers, while emphasizing his compassion for the average American, also agree he was vain, devious, and manipulative and had a passion for secrecy. These, they note, are often the standard weaknesses of great leaders. Significant social and political advances are made by those with drive, ambition, and a certain amount of brash, irrational self-confidence. . . .

Perhaps Dwight Eisenhower reconciled these clashing expectations better than recent presidents. Blessed with a wonderfully seductive, benign smile and a reserved, calming disposition, he was also the disciplined, strong, no-nonsense five-star general with all the medals and victories to go along with it. His ultimate resource as president was this reconciliation of decency and proven toughness, likability alongside demonstrated valor. Some of his biographers suggest his success was at least partly due to his uncanny ability to appear guileless to the public yet act with ample cunning in private. . . .

One of the ironies of the American presidency is that those characteristics we condemn in one president, we look for in another. Thus a supporter of Jimmy Carter's once suggested that Sunday school teacher Carter wasn't "rotten enough," "a wheeler-dealer," "an s.o.b."— precisely the virtues (if they can be called that) that Lyndon Johnson was most criticized for a decade earlier. President Clinton was viewed as both a gifted Southern Baptist–style preacher by some of his followers and a man who was character challenged, by opponents. . . .

Paradox #4. We admire the "above politics" nonpartisan or bipartisan approach, yet the presidency is perhaps the most political office in the American system, a system in which we need a creative entrepreneurial master politician.

The public yearns for a statesman in the White House, for a George Washington or a second "era of good feelings"— anything that might prevent partisanship or politics as usual in the White House. Former French President Charles de Gaulle once said, "I'm neither of the left nor of the right nor of the center, but above." In fact, however, the job of president demands that the officeholder be a gifted political broker, ever attentive to changing political moods and coalitions. . . .

Presidents are often expected to be above politics in some respects while being highly political in others. Presidents are never supposed to act with their eyes on the next election, yet their power position demands they must. They are neither supposed to favor any particular group or party nor wheel and deal and twist too many arms. That's politics and that's bad! Instead, a president is supposed to be "president of all the people," above politics. A president is also asked to lead a party, to help fellow party members get elected or reelected, to deal firmly with party barons, interest group chieftains, and congressional political brokers. His ability to gain legislative victories depends on his skills at party leadership and on the size of his party's congressional membership. Jimmy Carter once lamented that "It's very difficult for someone to serve in this office and meet the difficult issues in a proper and courageous way and still maintain a combination of interest-group approval that will provide a clear majority at election time."

To take the president out of politics is to assume, incorrectly, that a president will be generally right and the public generally wrong, that a president must be protected from the push and shove of political pressures. But what president has always been right? Over the years, public opinion has usually been as sober a guide as anything else on the political waterfront. And, lest we forget, having a president constrained and informed by public opinion is what democracy is all about.

The fallacy of antipolitics presidencies is that only one view of the national interest is tenable, and a president may pursue that view only by ignoring political conflict and pressure. Politics, properly conceived, is the art of accommodating the diversity and variety of public opinion to meet public goals. Politics is the task of building durable coalitions and majorities. It isn't always pretty. "The process isn't immaculate and cannot

always be kid-gloved. A president and his men must reward loyalty and punish opposition; it is the only way." . . .

Paradox #5. We want a president who can unify us, yet the job requires taking firm stands, making unpopular or controversial decisions that necessarily upset and divide us.

Closely related to paradox #4, paradox #5 holds that we ask the president to be a national unifier and a *harmonizer* while at the same time the job requires priority setting and *advocacy* leadership. The tasks are near opposites. . . .

Our nation is one of the few in the world that calls on its chief executive to serve as its symbolic, ceremonial head of state *and* as its political head of government. Elsewhere, these tasks are spread around. In some nations there is a monarch and a prime minister; in others there are three visible national leaders—a head of state, a premier, and a powerful party chief.

In the absence of an alternative office or institution, we demand that our president act as a unifying force in our lives. Perhaps it all began with George Washington, who so artfully performed this function. At least for a while he truly was above politics, a unique symbol of our new nation. He was a healer, a unifier, and an extraordinary man for several seasons. Today we ask no less of our presidents than that they should do as Washington did, and more.

We have designed a presidential job description, however, that often forces our contemporary presidents to act as national dividers. Presidents must necessarily divide when they act as the leaders of their political parties, when they set priorities to the advantage of certain goals and groups at the expense of others, when they forge and lead political coalitions, when they move out ahead of public opinion and assume the role of national educators, when they choose one set of advisers over another. A president, as a creative executive leader, cannot help but offend certain interests. When Franklin Roosevelt was running for a second term, some garment workers unfolded a great sign that said, "We love him for the enemies he has made." Such is the fate of a president on an everyday basis; if presidents choose to use power they will lose the goodwill of those who preferred inaction. . . .

Paradox #6. We expect our presidents to provide bold, visionary, innovative, *programmatic* leadership and at the same time to *pragmatically* respond to the will of public opinion majorities; that is to say, we expect presidents to lead and to follow, to exercise "democratic leadership."

We want both pragmatic and programmatic leadership. We want principled leadership and flexible, adaptable leaders. *Lead us,* but also *listen to us.*

Most people can be led only where they want to go. "Authentic leadership," wrote James MacGregor Burns, "is a collective process." It emerges from a sensitivity or appreciation of the motives and goals of both followers and leaders. The test of leadership, according to Burns, "is the realization of intended, real change that meets people's enduring needs." Thus a key function of leadership is "to engage followers, not merely to activate them, to commingle needs and aspirations and goals in a common enterprise, and in the process to make better citizens of both leaders and followers."

We want our presidents to offer leadership, to be architects of the future and to offer visions, plans, and goals. At the same time we want them to stay in close touch with the sentiments of the people. We want a certain amount of innovation, but we resist being led too far in any one direction.

We expect vigorous, innovative leadership when crises occur. Once a crisis is past, however, we frequently treat presidents as if we didn't need or want them around. We do expect presidents to provide us with bold, creative, and forceful initiatives "to move us ahead," but we resist radical new ideas and changes and usually embrace "new" initiatives only after they have achieved some consensus.

Most of our presidents have been conservatives or at best "pragmatic liberals." They have seldom ventured much beyond the crowd. They have followed public opinion rather than shaped it. John F. Kennedy, the author of the much-acclaimed *Profiles in Courage,* was often criticized for presenting more profile than courage.

He avoided political risks where possible. Kennedy was fond of pointing out that he had barely won election in 1960 and that great innovations should not be forced on the public by a leader with such a slender mandate. President Kennedy is often credited with encouraging widespread public participation in politics; but he repeatedly reminded Americans that caution is needed, that the important issues are complicated, technical, and best left to the administrative and political experts. Seldom did Kennedy attempt to change the political context in which he operated. Instead he resisted, "the new form of politics emerging with the civil rights movement: mass action, argument on social fundamentals, appeals to considerations of justice and morality. Moving the American political system in such a direction would necessarily have been long range, requiring arduous educational work and promising substantial political risk."

Kennedy, the pragmatist, shied away from such an unpragmatic undertaking. . . .

Paradox #7. Americans want powerful, self-confident presidential leadership. Yet we are inherently suspicious of leaders who are arrogant, infallible, and above criticism.

We unquestionably cherish our three branches of government with their checks and balances and theories of dispersed and separated powers. We want our presidents to be successful and to share their power with their cabinets, Congress, and other "responsible" national leaders. In theory, we oppose the concentration of power, we dislike secrecy, and we resent depending on any one person to provide all of our leadership.

But Americans also yearn for dynamic, aggressive presidents—even if they do cut some corners. We celebrate the gutsy presidents who make a practice of manipulating and pushing Congress. We perceive the great presidents to be those who stretched their legal authority and dominated the other branches of government. It is still Jefferson, Jackson, Lincoln, and the Roosevelts who get top billing. Whatever may have been the framers' intentions for the three branches, most experts now agree that most of the time, especially in crises, our system works best when the presidency is strong and when we have a self-confident, assertive president.

There is, of course, a fine line between confidence and arrogance, between firmness and inflexibility. We want presidents who are not afraid to exert their will, but at what point does this become antidemocratic, even authoritarian? . . .

Paradox #8. What it takes to become president may not be what is needed to govern the nation.

To win a presidential election takes ambition, money, luck, and masterful public relations strategies. It requires the formation of an electoral coalition. To govern a democracy requires much more. It requires the formation of a *governing* coalition, and the ability to compromise and bargain.

"People who win primaries may become good presidents—but 'it ain't necessarily so'" wrote columnist David Broder. "Organizing well is important in governing just as it is in winning primaries. But the Nixon years should teach us that good advance men do not necessarily make trustworthy White House aides. Establishing a government is a little more complicated than having the motorcade run on time."

Ambition (in heavy doses) and stiff-necked determination are essential for a presidential candidate, yet too much of either can be dangerous. A candidate must be bold and energetic, but in excess these characteristics can produce a cold, frenetic candidate. To win the presidency obviously requires a single-mindedness, yet our presidents must also have a sense of proportion, be well-rounded, have a sense of humor, be able to take a joke, and have hobbies and interests outside the realm of politics.

To win the presidency many of our candidates (Lincoln, Kennedy, and Clinton come to mind) had to pose as being more progressive or even populist than they actually felt; to be effective in the job they are compelled to appear more cautious and conservative than they often want to be. One of Carter's political strategists said, "Jimmy campaigned liberal but governed conservative." And as Bill Clinton pointed out toward the end of

his first year in office, "We've all become Eisenhower Republicans." . . .

We often also want both a "fresh face," an outsider, as a presidential candidate *and* a seasoned, mature, experienced veteran who knows the corridors of power and the back alleyways of Washington. That's why Colin Powell fascinated so many people. Frustration with past presidential performances leads us to turn to a "fresh new face" uncorrupted by Washington's politics and its "buddy system" (Carter, Reagan, Clinton). But inexperience, especially in foreign affairs, has sometimes led to blunders by the outsiders. . . .

Paradox #9. The presidency is sometimes too strong, yet other times too weak.

Presidents are granted wide latitude in dealing with events abroad. At times, presidents can act unilaterally, without the express consent of Congress. While the constitutional grounds for such action may be dubious, the climate of expectations allows presidents to act decisively abroad. This being the case, the public comes to think the president can do the same at home. But this is usually not the case. A clashing expectation is built into the presidency when strength in some areas is matched with weakness in other areas.

It often seems that our presidency is *always too strong* and *always too weak.* Always too powerful given our worst fears of tyranny and our ideals of a "government by the people." Always too strong, as well, because it now possesses the capacity to wage nuclear war (a capacity that doesn't permit much in the way of checks and balances and deliberative, participatory government). But always too weak when we remember nuclear, proliferation, the rising national debt, the budget deficit, lingering discrimination, poverty, and the clutch of other fundamental problems yet to be solved.

The presidency is always too strong when we dislike the incumbent! Its limitations are bemoaned, however, when we believe the incumbent is striving valiantly to serve the public interest as we define it. The Johnson presidency vividly captured this paradox: many who believed he was too strong in Vietnam also believed he was too weak to wage his War on Poverty. Others believed just the opposite. . . .

Ultimately, being paradoxical does not make the presidency incomprehensible. Can we rid the presidency of all paradoxes? We couldn't, even if we wanted to do so. And anyway, what is wrong with some ambiguity? It is in embracing the paradoxical nature of the American presidency that we may be able to arrive at understanding. And with understanding may come enlightened or constructive criticism. This is the basis for citizen democracy.

Chapter 10 Exercise

Choose three paradoxes noted by the authors and apply them to our current president. Do they match the presidents' behavior or are they not applicable?

Why is the presidency such a paradoxical office? Explain and provide examples to bolster your answer.

Part VII

Supreme Court

CHAPTER 11

Interpretation

"Who's Right about the Constitution?
Meese v. Brennan"

Stuart Taylor, Jr.

Stuart Taylor Jr. outlines the opposing perspectives of judicial activism and judicial restraint. He asks whether judges should defer to the founders' intentions—the position of former Attorney General Edwin Messe—or be guided by the communities' intention—the position favored by Justice Brennan. While these views could not be more different, they do highlight the importance of political judgment.

An activist jurisprudence, one which anchors the Constitution only in the consciences of jurists, is a chameleon jurisprudence, changing color and form in each era.

> The Constitution . . . is a mere thing of wax in the hands of the judiciary; which they may twist and shape into any form they please.

If the policy of the Government upon vital questions affecting the whole people is to be irrevocably fixed by decisions of the Supreme Court, the instant they are made . . . the people will have ceased to be their own rulers.

> The Court . . . has improperly set itself up as . . . a super-legislature . . . reading into the Constitution words and implications which are not there, and which were never intended to be there. . . . We want a Supreme Court which will do justice under the Constitution—not over it.

Sounds like Ed Meese, doesn't it? Well, the first quotation is the attorney general's. But the second comes from Thomas Jefferson, the third from Abraham Lincoln, and the fourth from Franklin D. Roosevelt. When Meese assails government by judiciary, he is in good company.

Meese has denounced major Supreme Court rulings of the past 60 years and called for judges to look to "the original meaning of constitutional provisions" as "the only reliable guide for judgment." No attorney general in the past four decades has set out so deliberately to reduce the power of the judiciary or to screen the ideological credentials of new appointees.

Champions of liberal judicial activism have launched a ferocious counterattack. Justices William J. Brennan Jr. and John Paul Stevens retorted with pointed critiques of Meese's so-called "jurisprudence of original intention." Brennan said it was "arrogance cloaked as humility" for anyone "to pretend that from our vantage we can gauge accurately the intent of the Framers on application of principle to specific, contemporary questions." The real animus of advocates of this "facile historicism" he said, is a "political" agenda hostile to the rights of minorities.

Meese is certainly vulnerable to this sort of attack. He seems less a constitutional philosopher than a constitutional window-shopper, seeking to dress up his conservative political agenda as a principled quest for truth. His notion that judges can answer the hard questions raised by the Constitution without being "tainted by ideological predilection," simply by plugging in the intent of the Framers, is at best simpleminded and at worst disingenuous. When the Framers' intentions *are* clear, but contrary to a result Meese wants, he ignores them. While calling for restraint in the exercise of judicial power—especially enforcement of civil liberties—he pushes to aggrandize executive power.

Along the way, he has said some revealing things. "You don't have many suspects who are innocent of a crime," he told *U.S. News & World Report.* "That's contradictory. If a person is innocent of a crime, then he is not a suspect." This from a man who was himself suspected of several federal crimes until a special prosecutor cleared him last year—a man who then billed the government $720,824.49 for his defense lawyers. (He later confessed to a "bad choice of words.")

Meese also assailed as "intellectually shaky" and "constitutionally suspect" the Court's 60-year-old doctrine that most of the Bill of Rights, originally applicable only to the national government, was applied to the states by the 14th Amendment. Eminent Supreme Court justices criticized the doctrine too, but that was decades ago. When a Supreme Court ruling has "been affirmed and reaffirmed through a course of years," Lincoln said in 1857, "it then might be, perhaps would be, factious, nay even revolutionary, not to acquiesce in it as a precedent."

Nevertheless, the standard liberal retort to Meese is superficial. It caricatures his position as more extreme than it is. It ignores the long and honorable history of political attacks on judicial usurpation of power. Most important, its scorn for the "original intention" approach begs the question of where—if not from those who wrote and ratified the Constitution and its amendments—unelected judges get a mandate to override the will of the political majority by striking down democratically enacted laws.

For all his fumbling, Meese has spotlighted some of the real problems with the freewheeling judicial activism sometimes practiced by people like Brennan. Among these is a tendency to "find" in the Constitution rights (such as abortion rights) and social policies that can honestly be found neither in the language of the document, nor in the records left by those who wrote it, nor in any broad national consensus that has evolved since then. This is bad constitutional law even when you like the policies, as I sometimes do.

Meese deserves credit for bringing the deepest questions of constitutional law out of the law journals and into the newspapers. He surely has a political motive. But liberals who believe in democracy (anybody out there after two Reagan landslides?) should welcome the debate.

Too often liberals have taken the elitist view that ordinary voters are the natural enemies of civil liberties, and that only judges can be trusted to protect them. It is a shortsighted approach. As Justice Robert Jackson said four decades ago, "Any court which undertakes by its legal processes to enforce civil liberties needs the support of an enlightened and vigorous public opinion." Today most people confine their thinking about the Constitution to whether they like the policies the Court has decreed. The larger question of when courts should displace the ordinary policy-making role of elected officials gets little attention from anyone but law professors. Meese has begun to remind the public that in enforcing constitutional rights, federal judges are by definition restraining majority rule.

Within proper limits this is a noble function. Those who wrote the Constitution and its amendments saw them as bulwarks against oppression of minorities by a tyrannical majority. They specified certain fundamental rights shared by all Americans. They created special protections for minorities, especially blacks. They laid down these principles in majestic generalities meant to have continuing relevance in a changing society—freedom of speech, equal protection of the laws, due process of law. The federal courts—precisely because they are not answerable to the voters—are the logical bodies to enforce these rights against the majority.

Here, however, lies a difficult dilemma to which no wholly satisfactory solution exists. The Constitution being what the judges say it is, how can the judges be prevented from usurping the powers of elected officials and making political decisions? Meese's admonition to stick to original intent is only a starting point. The Constitution does tell judges to enforce certain broad principles such as "freedom of speech," but if these principles are to be enforced at all in a changing society, judges must supply much of their meaning.

The trouble is that judges of all political stripes have gone beyond applying the Constitution's principles to new circumstances. They have written their own moral and political values into it, pretending to have found them there. Sometimes they have "interpreted" the Constitution to forbid things explicitly allowed by its language.

Take Brennan, a hero to liberals—deservedly so—and Meese's principal foil in the current debate. In his speech belittling "original intention" theorists, Brennan denied writing his own views into the Constitution. "It is, in a very real sense, the community's interpretation that is

sought," he said. "Justices are not platonic guardians appointed to wield authority according to their personal moral predilections."

But he gave these words a hollow ring when he explained why he always votes to strike down death penalty laws. He said they violate "the essential meaning" of the Eighth Amendment's prohibition against cruel and unusual punishment by denying "the intrinsic worth" of the murderers who are executed. Now, Brennan knows perfectly well that those who wrote that amendment had no intention of banning the death penalty, which was common at the time and was explicitly recognized in the Fifth and 14th Amendments.

So whence comes his mandate for invalidating the death penalty? "I hope to embody a community striving for human dignity for all, although perhaps not yet arrived," he explained. Translation: my moral convictions on this issue are so strong I would override the laws adopted by the people's elected representatives any way I could. Brennan admitted that most of his fellow countrymen and justices think the death penalty constitutional. As Judge Robert Bork has put it: "The truth is that the judge who looks outside the Constitution looks inside himself and nowhere else."

Well, what's so bad about that? If elected officials don't have the decency to end the death penalty (or antiabortion laws, or minimum-wage laws, or whatever else offends you), why shouldn't the judges do it?

The most important answer is that judicial legislation erodes democratic self-government. It converts judges into an unelected and illegitimate policy-making elite. Indeed, its more radical exponents evince a deep antipathy for the democratic process. But as Felix Frankfurter said, "Holding democracy in judicial tutelage is not the most promising way to foster disciplined responsibility in a people."

Defenders of judicial activism like to point out the vagueness of the Constitution's words and the futility of the quest for consensus on original intention. "And even if such a mythical beast could be captured and examined, how relevant would it be to us today?" asks Harvard law professor Laurence Tribe. He dismisses as a dangerous fallacy the notion that judges can be significantly restrained by the Constitution's text on history. The Supreme Court, he says, "just cannot avoid the painful duty of exercising judgment so as to give concrete meaning to the fluid Constitution."

Well, perhaps. But why can't the Court do something many law professors barely deign to discuss? When the Constitution's language and history provide little or no guidance on a subject, why can't it leave the law-making to legislatures? Those who work so hard to prove that the Constitution cannot supply the values for governance of modern society seem to think it follows that judges must do it, with a little help from their friends in academia. But their argument rebounds against the legitimacy of judicial review itself. Bork poses a question for which they have no good answer: "If the Constitution is not law—law that, with the usual areas of ambiguity around the edges, nevertheless tolerably tells judges what to do and what not to do— . . . what authorizes judges to set at naught the majority judgment of the American people?"

The activist approach of amending the Constitution in the guise of interpreting it goes hand in hand with a certain lack of candor about the enterprise. A judge who acknowledged that his goal was to strike down democratically adopted laws by rewriting the Constitution would risk impeachment. So we hear a lot about "finding" in the Constitution rights that had somehow gone unnoticed for more than a century.

There is no reason to suppose that unelected judges, using theories concocted by unelected law professors, will make better policies over time than elected officials. Nor that they will make more liberal policies. Judicial activism is not a game played only by liberals. Conservative judges rode roughshod over progressive and New Deal legislation for several decades ending about 1937. "Never . . . can the Supreme Court be said to have for a single hour been representative of anything except the relatively conservative forces of its day," Robert Jackson wrote in 1941.

Franklin Roosevelt changed that, ushering in an era of liberal judicial activism. Now the tables are turning again. Reagan and Meese are filling up the lower federal courts with conservatives and hoping to do the same with the Supreme Court. "I dream of a conservative Supreme Court striking down most federal legislation since the New Deal as unconstitutional," writes conservative columnist Joseph Sobran. Liberals may soon rediscover the virtues of judicial restraint, and find themselves urging a Reaganized judiciary to practice what Meese has been preaching.

Brennan and other liberal activist judges deserve the applause they have won for thrusting upon the nation some policies that were also triumphs of constitutional principle. Desegregation is one example. Protection of the rights of poor criminal defendants is another.

But liberal activism has gone to dubious extremes. Take the case of the man who approached a policeman in Denver and said he'd killed someone. The policeman told him about his rights to remain silent and have a lawyer. The man said he understood and proceeded with his confession, leading police to the scene where he said he had killed a 14-year-old girl. The sometime mental patient later told a psychiatrist that the voice of God had ordered him to confess. The Colorado Supreme Court threw out the confession on the ground that it was compelled by mental illness, and therefore involuntary. If he is ever tried, neither the confession nor, presumably, the other evidence ("fruits" of the confession) will be admissible. And he may go free.

Such judicial excesses are giving constitutional rights a bad name. Ed Meese is not alone in his outrage at judges who free criminals on the basis of technical rules that protect only the guilty, especially where they have little to do with deterring police abuse. The more this sort of thing happens, the greater the danger that the considerable public backlash may build to radical reaction.

There will always be cases in which judges must let criminals go free, and must defy public opinion, to vindicate the constitutional rights of innocent and guilty alike. Their ability to do so suffers when they squander the reservoir of good-will they need for such occasions. "Liberty lies in the hearts of men and women," Learned Hand wrote. "When it dies there, no constitution, no law, no court can save it."

Judicial creation of new constitutional rights can also be mistaken even when much or most of the public approves. The best example is *Roe v. Wade*, the 1973 decision creating a constitutional right to abortion and striking down all state antiabortion laws. Abortion is one of the toughest moral issues around. If I were a legislator I might vote (with misgivings) to allow free access to abortion in the early stages of pregnancy, as the Supreme Court did. But the Court is not a legislature, and there is no plausible basis in the Constitution for it to take this issue away from the states, some of which had already legalized abortion before *Roe*.

Justice Harry Blackmun's opinion "found" a right to abortion within the vague, general "right to personal privacy." He said these rights were in the Constitution somewhere, though he was not sure where—probably the 14th Amendment's generalized protection of "liberty," maybe the Ninth Amendment. Blackmun (appointed by Richard Nixon) made no pretense that the Framers of these amendments intended to legalize abortion. History shows clearly that they did not. They were not thinking about abortion at all, although it was a familiar practice, illegal in some states, when the 14th Amendment was adopted. Nor do the words of the Constitution provide a shred of support for the detailed regulations the Court has drafted over time to curb state regulation of abortion.

Right-to-lifers are not the only people who deplore *Roe v. Wade*. Many liberal scholars—defenders of the pioneering Warren Court decisions so despised by Meese—have said the Burger Court went too far down the road of naked judicial legislation in that case. Among them are Archibald Cox, now retired from Harvard Law School, Dean John Hart Ely of Stanford Law School, and Dean Benno Schmidt of Columbia Law School, soon to be president of Yale. The

abortion issue poses an excruciating clash between two moral imperatives: a woman's right to personal autonomy and protection of the unborn. Why every detail of local, state, and national policy on such a fundamental moral issue should depend on the personal philosophies of five or six judges escapes them, and me.

The disregard for the written Constitution that *Roe v. Wade* embodies is also a two-edged sword. President Reagan said in his debate with Walter Mondale that an unborn child is a living human being "protected by the Constitution, which guarantees life, liberty, and the pursuit of happiness to all of us." Well, there he goes again, quoting the Declaration of Independence and calling it the Constitution. But he was close enough; the 14th Amendment says no state may "deprive any person of life, liberty, or property, without due process of law." For those who believe a fetus is a "person" and abortion is murder, as Reagan does, it is possible to conclude that judges should strike down any state laws that allow it. Farfetched? Well, what if a state excluded homosexuals or handicapped children from the protection of its murder laws?

None of this means Meese's own approach to constitutional interpretation is adequate. It isn't. For starters, there is little evidence he has given the subject much thought. Beyond the high-sounding, platitudinous stuff about the Framers in the speeches his aides have written for him, he has had little specific to say about what he thinks their intentions were, or how broadly these intentions should be read. There is enormous room for disagreement here. The most important constitutional phrases, like "equal protection of the laws," are sweeping, vague, and only dimly illuminated by history.

Meese has tiptoed away from some of the few specific things he has said, including his attack on the doctrine that most of the Bill of Rights applies to the states through the 14th Amendment. It appeared in the written text of his July 9 speech to the American Bar Association. For some reason he omitted this point when he read the speech aloud. Moments afterward, reporters bearing tape recorders asked Meese whether he thought the Court had gone too far in applying the Bill of Rights to the states. "No," he responded. "I, well, I think this is something that's been done in 1925 and since, and so I don't think, ah, ah, I think, I do not have any particular quarrel at this stage of the game with what the Court has done in the intervening 60 years." Will the real Ed Meese please stand up?

Meese has stuck to his guns in denouncing as "infamous" major decisions upholding the rights of criminal defendants. One of his least favorites is *Mapp v. Ohio* (1961), which extended to the states the "exclusionary rule" barring use of evidence seized in violation of the Fourth Amendment. Meese has said *Mapp* helps only "the guilty criminal," and has suggested abandoning the exclusionary rule in state and federal cases alike.

But Meese seems to have forgotten *Boyd v. U.S.*, which Justice Louis Brandeis said "will be remembered as long as civil liberty lives in the United States." The 1886 decision was the Supreme Court's first major Fourth and Fifth Amendment ruling. Unlike modern rulings, it was explicitly based on a detailed study of the Framers' intentions. *Boyd* held that the Framers intended the Fourth Amendment's ban on "unreasonable searches and seizures" to prohibit *all* governmental attempts to obtain a person's private papers or other property—even by warrant or subpoena—and to forbid their use as evidence to convict him. Innocence or guilt was irrelevant to this determination. The Court's confident assertion that this was the Framers' intention was based on a reading of their natural rights philosophy, on 18th-century case law, and on the fury at sweeping British searches that helped fuel the American Revoluton.

If *Boyd* were the law today, it would place far greater restrictions on police than any imposed by the Warren Court, which Meese has denounced for its "expansive civil liberatarianism." The modern Court, unwilling to restrict official power so severely, has abandoned this broad vision. Its use of the exclusionary rule as a lim-

ited deterrent to police abuses is a pale remnant of the expansive rights the Court saw in the Fourth Amendment 99 years ago.

Meese's contention that the exclusionary rule helps only guilty criminals is demonstrably false. Of course, exclusion of improperly obtained but reliable evidence helps only the guilty in the immediate case at hand. But if officials knew they could search everyone indiscriminately and use any evidence they found, a lot of innocent people would be victims of illegal searches. The only way to take the profit out of police abuses is to bar use of the evidence found. This means letting some guilty criminals go free. It is one thing to say this is too high a price to pay in cases in which police inadvertently cross the line between marginally legal and marginally illegal searches. It is quite another to let officials use any and all illegally obtained evidence, as Meese would.

Meese's selectiveness in applying original intention is not limited to criminal law issues. If he really believed the Framers' specific intentions are "the only reliable guide for judgment," he would have to condemn *Brown v. Board of Education*, the landmark 1954 decision desegregating public schools. Anybody who did that today would be assailed as a segregationist crank. Meese recently applauded *Brown* as a case study in finding the original intention of the post–Civil War 14th Amendment. "The Supreme Court in that case was not giving new life to old words, or adapting a 'living,' 'flexible' Constitution to new reality," he declared. "It was restoring the original principle of the Constitution."

That's nice, but it's not true. The Congress that wrote the amendment had no intention of outlawing segregation, as Raoul Berger, Alexander Bickel, and others have demonstrated. The same Congress segregated its own Senate gallery and the District of Columbia schools, and rejected various desegregation bills. What the Court saw nearly 90 years later was that state-enforced segregation, relegating blacks to inferior schools and other facilities, had made a mockery of the 14th Amendment's central purpose: to put blacks and whites on an equal footing before the law. So the

Court gave "new life to old words," to use Meese's mocking phrase, and threw out segregation.

The same Congress that drafted the 14th Amendment also passedsome special welfare programs for recently freed slaves and other blacks in the South. These were, in modern parlance, affirmative action programs involving racial preferences, for blacks—sort of like the government hiring quotas that Meese has declared in violation of the 14th Amendment. Congress specifically excluded whites from some of these programs. Among them were federally funded, racially segregated schools for blacks only—a single program that contradicts the Meese view of the 14th Amendment's original intention on segregation and affirmative action alike. These programs were passed over the Meese-like objections that they discriminated against whites and included some blacks who were not personally victims of discrimination. But Meese's Justice Department, checking its slogans about judicial restraint at the door, has urged the Supreme Court to strike down every local, state, and federal government affirmative action program in the nation that prefers black employees over whites. Right or wrong, Meese's position on affirmative action is at war with his preachings about strict adherence to original intention.

The same is true of his position on a lot of issues. Many of the powers that his Justice Department exercises daily—reaching into every community with its wiretaps, its informers, its subpoenas—would have horrified the Framers. They feared centralized power more than anything but anarchy. They sought to limit severely the national government's law enforcement powers, leaving to state and local authorities jurisdiction over the all but genuinely interstate crimes.

What would Meese do about the strong historical evidence that the Framers intended to deny the government the power to issue paper money, which they saw as a threat to propertied interests? What about their intent to bar the president from launching military expeditions without congressional approval, except to repel attacks on United States territory?

And what about the First Amendment's religion clauses, as expounded by Joseph Story, a 19th-century justice whom Meese sometimes quotes on original intention? "The real object," Story said, "was not to countenance, much less to advance, Mahometanism, or Judaism, or infidelity, by prostrating Christianity; but to exclude all rivalry among Christian sects." Meese buys the "infidels" part when he says the Framers would have found "bizarre" the notion that government may not favor religion over nonreligion. He ignores the rest, of course. Any official who argued today that only Christians are protected by the religion clauses would be drummed out of office, and properly so.

The broader point is that sticking to the Framers' immediate goals as closely as Meese sometimes suggests is neither possible nor desirable. If *Brown v. Board of Education* was right, and it was, then a "jurisprudence of original intention" worthy of respect cannot mean enforcing constitutional rights only in the specific ways envisioned by the Framers. Such an approach would doom these rights to wither with the passage of time. The Framers' central purpose of preventing abuse of minorities would be strangled by narrow-minded attention to their more immediate concerns. As for the possibility of updating the Constitution by the formal amendment process, this takes a two-thirds majority in each house of Congress and approval by three-fourths of the states. Such majorities could rarely be mustered to deal with new threats to the rights of minorities.

New technologies such as wiretapping threaten liberties the Framers enshrined in ways that they could not have imagined. And the changing nature of society poses threats that the Framers did not foresee to the constitutional principles they established. Take libel law. Million-dollar libel suits by public officials were not prevalent in the 18th century, and it is fairly dear that the Framers did not intend the First Amendment (or the 14th) to limit private libel suits as the modern Court has done. But they did intend to protect uninhibited, robust, and wide-open debate about public affairs. And it seems to me proper for the Supreme Court to effectuate that broad purpose, in this litigious era, by imposing some curbs on libel suits.

Am I slipping into the kind of judicial revision of the Constitution I just rejected? I don't think so. There is a middle ground between narrow adherence to original intention and free-wheeling judicial legislation. As Chief Justice John Marshall said in a famous 1819 decision, the Constitution is not a code of "immutable rules," but rather the "great outlines" of a system intended "to endure for ages to come, and, consequently, to be adapted to the various crises of human affairs." But it is for elected officials, as he said, to do most of the adapting. Judges should invalidate democratically enacted laws only, in John Ely's words, "in accord with an inference whose starting point, whose underlying premise, is fairly discoverable in the Constitution."

This approach will often set only loose outer boundaries around the Court's options in deciding specific issues. It requires judges in close cases to draw fine lines. And it does not pretend to purge their moral and political convictions entirely from the process. But its recognition that the Constitution imposes some bounds on judicial power—limits fleshed out more clearly by the accumulation of precedent—would channel the growth of the law in a more principled and therefore more legitimate direction.

At the outer limits of legitimacy are those cases in which the justices read into vague constitutional phrases like "due process" an emerging social consensus that seems contrary to the particular intentions of the Framers. This goes beyond applying old principles to new circumstances and gets into tinkering with the principles or creating new ones. I think the Supreme Court should do it in a few rare cases, nudging society to progress in the common law tradition of gradually evolving principles against a background of continuity.

Brown v. Board of Education was such a case. It struck at the heart of a great evil. Though departing from the particular plans of the Framers honored their deeper, nobler intentions. And though overriding the democratic process, it crystallized an emerging national consensus that legally compelled racial segregation was unacceptable in modern America. That is the difference between judicial activism and judicial statesmanship, and why most of the fiercest critics of judicial activism don't dare criticize *Brown* today.

But the Court should attempt to lead only where the nation is prepared to follow. The creation of new constitutional values is a slippery slope, down which the courts should not travel too far too fast. At the bottom lies the kind of uninhibited and essentially lawless judicial legislation that Bork has justly assailed. The urge to do good is powerful, the urge to court greatness intoxicating. Judges should resist the sincere, but arrogant, assumption that they know best. Brandeis's words, aimed at Ed Meese's ideological predecessors, should also be heeded by his ideological adversaries: "The greatest danger to liberty is the insidious encroachment by men of zeal, well-meaning but without understanding."

Chapter 11 Exercise

Define and discuss the differences between judicial activism and judicial restraint.

Identify and discuss the proper role of the judiciary in our democracy.

PART VIII

Public Opinion and Media

CHAPTER 12

Informed Citizens

The Phantom Public

Walter Lippmann

In this passage from *The Phantom Public,* Walter Lippmann portrays the public as relatively uninformed, disinterested in public matters, and often inconsistent in their political views. The ideal of public opinion, according to Lippmann, "is to align men during the crisis of a problem in such a way as to favor the action of those individuals who may be able to compose the crisis."

The private citizen today has come to feel rather like a deaf spectator in the back row, who ought to keep his mind on the mystery off there, but cannot quite manage to keep awake. He knows he is somehow affected by what is going on. Rules and regulations continually, taxes annually and wars occasionally remind him that he is being swept along by great drifts of circumstance.

Yet these public affairs are in no convincing way his affairs. They are for the most part invisible. They are managed, if they are managed at all, at distant centers, from behind the scenes, by unnamed powers. As a private person he does not know for certain what is going on, or who is doing it, or where he is being carried. No newspaper reports his environment so that he can grasp it; no

school has taught him how to imagine it; his ideals, often, do not fit with it; listening to speeches, uttering opinions and voting do not, he finds, enable him to govern it. He lives in a world which he cannot see, does not understand and is unable to direct.

In the cold light of experience he knows that his sovereignty is a fiction. He reigns in theory, but in fact he does not govern. . . .

There is then nothing particularly new in the disenchantment which the private citizen expresses by not voting at all, by voting only for the head of the ticket, by staying away from the primaries, by not reading speeches and documents, by the whole list of sins of omission for which he is denounced. I shall not denounce him further. My sympathies are with him, for I believe that he has been saddled with an impossible task and that he is asked to practice an unattainable ideal. I find it so myself for, although public business is my main interest and I give most of my time to watching it, I cannot find time to do what is expected of me in the theory of democracy; that is, to know what is going on and to have an opinion worth expressing on every question which confronts a self-governing community. And I have not happened to meet anybody, from a President of the United States to a professor of political science, who came anywhere near to embodying the accepted ideal of the sovereign and omnicompetent citizen. . . .

[Today's theories] assume that either the voters are inherently competent to direct the course of affairs or that they are making progress toward such an ideal. I think it is a false ideal. I do not mean an undesirable ideal. I mean an unattainable ideal, bad only in the sense that it is bad for a fat man to try to be a ballet dancer. An ideal should express the true possibilities of its subject. When it does not it perverts the true possibilities. The ideal of the omnicompetent, sovereign citizen is, in my opinion, such a false ideal. It is unattainable. The pursuit of it is misleading. The failure to achieve it has produced the current disenchantment.

The individual man does not have opinions on all public affairs. He does not know how to direct public affairs. He does not know what is happening, why it is happening, what ought to happen. I cannot imagine how he could know, and there is not the least reason for thinking, as mystical democrats have thought, that the compounding of individual ignorances in masses of people can produce a continuous directing force in public affairs. . . .

The need in the Great Society not only for publicity but for uninterrupted publicity is indisputable. But we shall misunderstand the need seriously if we imagine that the purpose of the publication can possibly be the informing of every voter. We live at the mere beginnings of public accounting. Yet the facts far exceed our curiosity. . . . A few executives here and there . . .

read them. The rest of us ignore them for the good and sufficient reason that we have other things to do. . . .

Specific opinions give rise to immediate executive acts; to take a job, to do a particular piece of work, to hire or fire, to buy or sell, to stay here or go there, to accept or refuse, to command or obey. General opinions give rise to delegated, indirect, symbolic, intangible results: to a vote, to a resolution, to applause, to criticism, to praise or dispraise, to audiences, circulations, followings, contentment or discontent. The specific opinion may lead to a decision to act within the area where a man has personal jurisdiction, that is, within the limits set by law and custom, his personal power and his personal desire. But general opinions lead only to some sort of expression, such as voting, and do not result in executive acts except in cooperation with the general opinions of large numbers of other persons.

Since the general opinions of large numbers of persons are almost certain to be a vague and confusing medley, action cannot be taken until these opinions have been factored down, canalized, compressed and made uniform. . . . The making of one general will out of a multitude of general wishes . . . consists essentially in the use of symbols which assemble emotions after they have been detached from their ideas. Because feelings are much less specific than ideas, and yet more poignant, the leader is able to make a homogeneous will out of a heterogeneous mass of desires. The process, therefore, by which general opinions are brought to cooperation consists of an intensification of feeling and a degradation of significance. Before a mass of general opinions can eventuate in executive action, the choice is narrowed down to a few alternatives. The victorious alternative is executed not by the mass but by individuals in control of its energy. . . .

We must assume, then, that the members of a public will not possess an insider's knowledge of events or share his point of view. They cannot, therefore, construe intent, or appraise the exact circumstances, enter intimately into the minds of the actors or into the details of the argument. They can watch only for coarse signs indicating where their sympathies ought to turn.

We must assume that the members of a public will not anticipate a problem much before its crisis has become obvious, nor stay with the problem long after its crisis is past. They will not know the antecedent events, will not have seen the issue as it developed, will not have thought out or willed a program, and will not be able to predict the consequences of acting on that program. We must assume as a theoretically fixed premise of popular government that normally men as members of a public will not be well informed, continuously interested, nonpartisan, creative or executive. We must assume that a public is inexpert in its curiosity, intermittent, that it discerns only gross distinctions, is slow to be aroused and quickly diverted; that, since it acts by aligning itself, it personalizes whatever it considers, and is interested only when events have been melodramatized as a conflict.

The public will arrive in the middle of the third act and will leave before the last curtain, having stayed just long enough perhaps to decide who is the hero and who the villain of the piece. Yet usually that judgment will necessarily be made apart from the intrinsic merits, on the basis of a sample of behavior, an aspect of a situation, by very rough external evidence. . . .

. . . The ideal of public opinion is to align men during the crisis of a problem in such a way as to favor the action of those individuals who may be able to compose the crisis. The power to discern those individuals is the end of the effort to educate public opinion. . . .

Public opinion, in this theory, is a reserve of force brought into action during a crisis in public affairs. Though it is itself an irrational force, under favorable institutions, sound leadership and decent training the power of public opinion might be placed at the disposal of those who stood for workable law as against brute assertion. In this theory, public opinion does not make the law. But by canceling lawless power it may establish the condition under which law can be made. It does not reason, investigate, invent, persuade, bargain or settle. But, by holding the aggressive

party in check, it may liberate intelligence. Public opinion in its highest ideal will defend those who are prepared to act on their reason against the interrupting force of those who merely assert their will.

That, I think, is the utmost that public opinion can effectively do. With the substance of the problem it can do nothing usually but meddle ignorantly or tyrannically. . . .

For when public opinion attempts to govern directly it is either a failure or a tyranny. It is not able to master the problem intellectually, nor to deal with it except by wholesale impact. The theory of democracy has not recognized this truth because it has identified the functioning of government with the will of the people. This is a fiction. The intricate business of framing laws and of administering them through several hundred thousand public officials is in no sense the act of the voters nor a translation of their will. . . .

Therefore, instead of describing government as an expression of the people's will, it would seem better to say that government consists of a body of officials, some elected, some appointed, who handle professionally, and in the first instance, problems which come to public opinion spasmodically and on appeal. Where the parties directly responsible do not work out an adjustment, public officials intervene. When the officials fail, public opinion is brought to bear on the issue. . . .

This, then, is the ideal of public action which our inquiry suggests. Those who happen in any question to constitute the public should attempt only to create an equilibrium in which settlements can be reached directly and by consent. The burden of carrying on the work of the world, of inventing, creating, executing, of attempting justice, formulating laws and moral codes, of dealing with the technic and the substance, lies not upon public opinion and not upon government but on those who are responsibly concerned as agents in the affair. Where problems arise, the ideal is a settlement by the particular interests involved. They alone know what the trouble really is. No decision by public officials or by commuters reading headlines in the train can usually and in the long run be so good as settlement by consent among the parties at interest. No moral code, no political theory can usually and in the long run be imposed from the heights of public opinion, which will fit a case so well as direct agreement reached where arbitrary power has been disarmed.

It is the function of public opinion to check the use of force in a crisis, so that men, driven to make terms, may live and let live.

Chapter 12 Exercise

According to Lippmann, what is public opinion?

Is Lippmann optimistic or critical of the role of citizens in government decision-making? Explain.

CHAPTER 13

Niche Media

The Massless Media

William Powers

William Powers summarizes the recent changes in the mass media and compares them to prior periods of change in our political history. Though he does not view changes as necessarily bad for democracy, Powers does believe that the increasingly diverse and niche-oriented news media of today parallels the partisan media of the 19th century.

One day last June, as a hot political summer was just warming up, a new poll was released. This one wasn't about which candidate voters favored for the White House. It was about which news channels they were choosing with their TV remotes.

"Political polarization is increasingly reflected in the public's news viewing habits," the Pew Research Center for the People and the Press reported.

> Since 2000, the Fox News Channel's gains have been greatest among political conservatives and Republicans. More than half of regular Fox viewers describe themselves as politically conservative (52%), up from 40% four years ago. At the same time, CNN, Fox's principal rival, has a more Democrat-leaning audience than in the past.

It's no surprise, of course, that Fox News viewers are more conservative than CNN viewers. But it is rather surprising that even as the network's audience is growing in sheer numbers, it is also growing increasingly conservative. The months following the poll offered further evidence of the ideological sorting of cable-news viewers. During the Democratic National Convention, in July, CNN came in first in the cable ratings, prompting a Fox spokesman to say, "They were playing to their core audience." Weeks later, during the Republican National Convention, Fox News played to *its* core audience and scored ratings that beat not only CNN and the other cable channels but even the broadcast networks—a historical first. When election day came around and George Bush won, it wasn't hard to predict that

Fox News would again be the cable ratings victor: the conservative candidate took the prize, and so, naturally, did the news channel favored by conservatives.

Committed partisans on the left and the right have always had ideological media outlets they could turn to (*The Nation* and *National Review*, for example), but for most Americans political affiliation was not the determining factor in choosing where they got their news. The three national networks, CBS, NBC, and ABC, offered pretty much the same product and the same establishment point of view. That product was something you shared with all Americans—not just friends, neighbors, and others like you but millions of people you would never meet, many of them very unlike you.

For some time now Americans have been leaving those vast media spaces where they used to come together and have instead been clustering in smaller units. The most broad-based media outlets, the networks and metropolitan newspapers, have been losing viewers and readers for years. But lately, thanks to the proliferation of new cable channels and the rise of digital and wireless technology, the disaggregation of the old mass audience has taken on a furious momentum. And the tribalization is not just about political ideology. In the post-mass-media era audiences are sorting themselves by ethnicity, language, religion, profession, socioeconomic status, sexual orientation, and numerous other factors.

"The country has atomized into countless market segments defined not only by demography, but by increasingly nuanced and insistent product preferences," *Business Week* reported last July, in a cover story called "The Vanishing Mass Market." To survive in this environment even old mass-media companies have had to learn the art of "niching down." Though national magazines have produced targeted subeditions for years, the slicing grows ever thinner. Time, Inc., the granddaddy of print media for the masses, has launched a new women's magazine just for Wal-Mart shoppers. Radio now has satellite and Web variants that let listeners choose their taste pods with exceptional precision. The fast-growing XM

Satellite Radio has not just one "urban" music channel but seven, each serving up a different subgenre twenty-four hours a day.

Some niches are so small they're approaching the vanishing point. There are now hundreds of thousands of bloggers, individuals who publish news, commentary, and other content on their own idiosyncratic Web sites. Some boast readerships exceeding those of prestigious print magazines, but most number their faithful in the double and triple digits. Find the one who shares your tastes and leanings, and you'll have attained the ne plus ultra of bespoke media: the ghostly double of yourself.

To sensibilities shaped by the past fifty years, the emerging media landscape seems not just chaotic but baleful. Common sense would suggest that as the vast village green of the broadcast era is chopped up into tiny plots, divisions in the culture will only multiply. If everyone tunes in to a different channel, and discourse happens only among like minds, is there any hope for social and political cohesion? Oh, for a cozy living room with one screen and Walter Cronkite signing off with his authoritative, unifying "That's the way it is."

It's instructive to remember, however, that the centralized, homogeneous mass-media environment of Cronkite's day was really an anomaly, an exception to the historical rule. For two centuries before the arrival of television America had a wild, cacophonous, emphatically *de*centralized media culture that mirrored society itself. And something like that media culture seems to be returning right now.

When primitive newspapers first appeared in seventeenth-century London, they were just official bulletins about the doings of the monarchy. Royally sanctioned and censored, they had no ideology other than that of the throne. The first real American newspaper, the *Boston News-Letter*, came straight from this mold. It was put out by an imperial official, the postmaster of colonial Boston, and stamped with the same seal of governmental approval worn by its British predecessors: "Published by Authority."

That timid approach didn't last long in America, however. In 1721 a Boston printer named James Franklin, older brother of Benjamin, founded a paper called the *New England Courant,* which brashly questioned the policies of the colony's ruling elite. The very first issue attacked Cotton Mather and other worthies for their support of smallpox inoculations. The paper was on the wrong side of that argument, but the real news was that it made the argument at all. The *Courant* was "America's first fiercely independent newspaper, a bold, antiestablishment journal that helped to create the nation's tradition of an irreverent press," Walter Isaacson writes in his recent biography of Benjamin Franklin (whose first published writings appeared in his brother's paper).

Franklin's paper set the tone for the evolution of the media in this country. Outspoken newspapers played a crucial role in the Revolutionary War, and when it was over the leaders of the young republic consciously used public policy to nurture a free press. As the Princeton sociologist Paul Starr notes in his recent book, *The Creation of the Media: Political Origins of Modern Communications,* the United States dispensed with the European tradition of licensing papers and policing their content. Congress even granted American publishers lower rates for postal delivery, a valuable subsidy that made starting up and running a paper more economical.

Such policies, combined with the freewheeling ethos that had already taken root in the press, set off a wild journalistic flowering in the nineteenth century. By the 1830s newspapers were everywhere, and they spoke in a myriad of voices about all manner of issues. Alexis de Tocqueville, who was accustomed to the reined-in newspapers of France, marveled at all the variety.

> The number of periodical and semi-periodical publications in the United States is almost incredibly large . . . It may readily be imagined that neither discipline nor unity of action can be established among so many combatants, and each one consequently fights under his own standard. All the political journals of the United States are, indeed, arrayed on the side of the administration or against it; but they attack and defend it in a thousand different ways.

In this the media reflected the political scene. The nineteenth century was a time of intense national growth and fervent argument about what direction the country should take. Numerous political parties appeared (Democratic, Whig, Republican, Free Soil, Know-Nothing), and the views and programs they advocated all found expression in sympathetic papers. In fact, the parties themselves financially supported newspapers, as did the White House for a time. Starr notes that according to a U.S. Census estimate, by the middle of the nineteenth century 80 percent of American newspapers were avowedly partisan.

This partisanship was not typically expressed in high-minded appeals to readers' better instincts. As Tocqueville wrote, "The characteristics of the American journalist consist in an open and coarse appeal to the passions of his readers; he abandons principles to assail the characters of individuals, to track them into private life and disclose all their weaknesses and vices." When Martin Chuzzlewit, the central character of the Dickens novel by the same name, arrives in the New York City of the early 1840s, he is greeted by newsboys hawking papers with names like the *New York Stabber* and the *New York Keyhole Reporter.* "Here's the *New York Sewer!,*" one newsie shouts. "Here's the *Sewer*'s exposure of the Wall Street Gang, and the *Sewer*'s exposure of the Washington Gang, and the *Sewer*'s exclusive account of a flagrant act of dishonesty committed by the Secretary of State when he was eight years old."

Yet even though the media of this period were profuse, partisan, and scandalously downmarket, they were at the same time a powerful amalgamator that encouraged participatory democracy and forged a sense of national identity. Michael Schudson, a professor of communication and sociology at the University of California at San Diego and the author of *The Sociology of News* (2003), says that the rampant partisanship displayed by newspapers "encouraged people to be attentive to their common enterprise of electing representatives or presidents." Commenting that "politics was the best entertainment in town in the middle of the 19th century," Schudson compares its effect to that of sports today.

"Professional baseball is an integrative mechanism even though it works by arousing very partisan loyalties," he says. In other words, newspapers helped pull the country together not by playing down differences and pretending everyone agreed but by celebrating and exploiting the fact that people didn't. It's the oldest American paradox: nothing unifies like individualism.

We tend to think of the rise of the modern mass media as primarily a function of technology: the advent of television, for example, enabled broadcasters to reach tens of millions of Americans, but the cost of entry was high enough to sharply limit the number of networks. However, technology was only one of several factors that determined the character of the media establishment that arose in the United States after World War II. Beginning in the nineteenth century the idea of objectivity began to cross over from science into business and popular culture. As the historian Scott Sandage notes in his new book, *Born Losers: A History of Failure in America,* a whole new industry rose up in nineteenth-century New York when a handful of creative entrepreneurs discovered they could gather "objective" information about businesses and people (the precursor of modern-day credit ratings) and sell it to other businesses for a profit. Soon journalists, including the muckrakers of the Progressive Era, were embracing a similar notion of objective, irrefutable fact. When the Washington journalist Walter Lippmann wrote in the 1920s that "good reporting requires the exercise of the highest of scientific virtues," and called for the founding of journalistic research institutes, he was, as Starr notes, codifying a standard of disinterested inquiry that would influence generations of journalists to come.

At the same time, a federal government that had once used policy to encourage the growth of a free press now faced a very different challenge. Unlike newspapers, the public airwaves were a finite resource, and someone had to decide how to dole it out. The solution was a federal regulatory structure that sought to ensure fairness but could never offer the ease of access or the expressive

freedom of the press. (Not that the networks necessarily wanted the latter; in order to pull in the large audiences that ad buyers demanded, all strove for a safe neutrality that offended no one.) For these reasons, although the broadcast media reached more people, the range of content they offered was actually more constricted than that of the print media that preceded them.

Finally, the political culture of the 1940s and 1950s discouraged extremism. The two major political parties of that period certainly had their differences, but they shared a basic set of beliefs about the country's priorities. Politics hewed to the center, and the media both reflected and reinforced this tendency. The centrist, "objective" networks and large newspapers didn't just *cover* the political establishment; they were an essential part of it. The anchormen who appeared on television and the columnists of the great papers were effectively spokesmen for the ruling postwar elite. (On occasion literally so: Lippmann, the great proponent of objectivity, worked with his fellow reporter James Reston on a famous speech by Senator Arthur Vandenberg; both journalists then turned around to write about the speech for their respective papers.)

That establishment consensus exploded in the 1960s and 1970s, with Vietnam and Watergate, but the mass media hung on for a few decades, a vestigial reminder of what had been. The Reagan era and the end of the Cold War dealt the old politico-media structure the final blows. In the 1990s partisan politics really took hold in Washington, and again the news media followed suit. The demise of the postwar consensus made the mass media's centrism obsolete. Long-simmering conservative resentment of the mainstream media fueled the rise of Rush Limbaugh and Fox News. Their success, in turn, has lately inspired efforts on the left to create avowedly liberal radio and cable outlets.

Socially, too, our fragmented media are to this era what James Franklin's newspaper was to the 1720s and the CBS evening news was to the 1950s. The cultural sameness and conformity that prevailed after World War II—the era of *Father Knows Best* and Betty Crocker—have been replaced by a popular pursuit of difference and self-expression. In explaining why McDonald's has shifted a significant portion of its advertising into niches, an executive of the company told *BusinessWeek,* "From the consumer point of view, we've had a change from 'I want to be normal' to 'I want to be special.' In a mass-media world it's hard to be special. But in the land of niches it's easy. What is blogging if not a celebration of the self?

The "Trust us, we know better" ethos that undergirded the broadcast era today seems increasingly antique. If red and blue America agree on anything, it's that they don't believe the media. To traditionalists worried about the future of news, this attitude reflects a corrosive cynicism. But in another way it's much like the skepticism that animates great journalism. As the media have become more transparent, and suffered their own scandals, the public has learned to think about the news the same way a good journalist would—that is, to doubt everything it's told.

Although network ratings continue to plummet, there's still evidence elsewhere of an enduring demand for the sort of connectedness that only broad-based media can offer. For the six months that ended last September 30 many of America's largest newspapers saw the now customary declines in circulation. But among those that saw increases were the only three with a national subscriber base: *The New York Times, The Wall Street Journal,* and *USA Today.* The presidential debates last year drew impressive audiences to the broadcast networks, suggesting that although Americans no longer go to mass outlets out of habit, they will go by choice when there's good reason. In one of those debates Senator John Kerry cracked a Tony Soprano joke, and it was safe to assume that most viewers got the allusion. When we rue the passing of mass togetherness, we often forget that the strongest connective tissue in modern culture is entertainment—a mass medium if ever there was one.

Moreover, for all the pointed criticism and dismissive eye-rolling that niche and mass outlets direct each other's way, the two are becoming more and more symbiotic. Where would the *Drudge Report* and the blogging horde be without *The New York Times, CBS News,* and *The Washington Post?* Were it not for the firsthand reporting offered by those media dinosaurs, the Internet crowd would have nothing to talk about. Conversely, where would the Web versions of mass outlets be without the traffic that is directed their way by the smaller players? If there's a new media establishment taking form, it's shaped like a pyramid, with a handful of mass outlets at the top and innumerable niches supporting them from below, barking upward.

Whenever critics of the new media worry about the public's clustering in niches, there's an unspoken assumption that viewers watch only one outlet, as was common thirty years ago—that is, that there are Fox people and CNN people, and never the twain shall meet. But the same Pew poll that showed the increasingly ideological grouping of cable audiences revealed that most Americans watch the news with remote at the ready, poised to dart away at any moment. Pew also detected an enormous affinity for "inadvertent" news consumption: a large majority of Internet users from almost all demographic groups say that while online they encounter news unexpectedly, when they aren't even looking for it. "Fully 73% of Internet users come across the news this way," Pew reported, "up from 65% two years ago, and 55% as recently as 1999." Thus it appears that one of the great joys of newspaper reading—serendipitous discovery—lives on.

And although much changes in the media over time, there are some eternal truths. Most outlets crave two things, money and impact, and the easiest path to both is the old-fashioned one: grow your audience. Ambitious niches will always seek to become larger, and in so doing to attract a more diverse audience. It's only a matter of time before the first mass blog is identified, celebrated, and showered with minivan ads.

Finally, there's no substantive evidence yet that the rise of the niches is bad for democracy. The fractious, disunited, politically partisan media of the nineteenth century heightened public awareness of politics, and taught the denizens of a new democracy how to be citizens. Fast forward to the present. The United States just held an election that was covered by noisy, divisive, often thoroughly disreputable post-broadcast-era media. And 120 million people, 60 percent of eligible voters, showed up to cast their ballots—a higher percentage than have voted in any election since 1968. Maybe we're on to something.

Chapter 13 Exercise

Describe the changes in the news media over the past several decades and identify and discuss potential political consequences of such change.

PART IX

Elections

CHAPTER 14

Rational Voters

Democratic Practice and Democratic Theory

Bernard R. Berelson, Paul F. Lazarsfeld, and William N. McPhee

This passage from the classic *Voting* details the limitations of voters and the requirements of democratic systems. Perhaps, surprisingly, the authors observe that the very limitations of many voters make our political system stronger, more dynamic, and less likely to move toward extremity. Though we cannot safely characterize voters as rational they nevertheless possess a diversity of characteristics that are vital to a successful democracy.

Requirements for the Individual

Perhaps the main impact of realistic research on contemporary politics has been to temper some of the requirements set by our traditional normative theory for the typical citizen. "Out of all this literature of political observation and analysis, which is relatively new," says Max Beloff, "there has come to exist a picture in our minds of the political scene which differs very considerably from that familiar to us from the classical texts of democratic politics."

Experienced observers have long known, of course, that the individual voter was not all that the theory of democracy requires of him. As

[British Lord James] Bryce put it [in his 1888 treatise, *The American Commonwealth*]:

> How little solidity and substance there is in the political or social beliefs of nineteen persons out of every twenty. These beliefs, when examined, mostly resolve themselves into two or three prejudices and aversions, two or three prepossessions for a particular party or section of a party, two or three phrases or catch-words suggesting or embodying arguments which the man who repeats them has not analyzed.

While our data do not support such an extreme statement, they do reveal that certain requirements commonly assumed for the successful operation of democracy are not met by the behavior of the "average" citizen. The requirements, and our conclusions concerning them, are quickly reviewed.

Interest, Discussion, Motivation

The democratic citizen is expected to be interested and to participate in political affairs. His interest and participation can take such various forms as reading and listening to campaign materials, working for the candidate or the party, arguing politics, donating money, and voting. . . . Many vote without real involvement in the election, and even the party workers are not typically motivated by ideological concerns or plain civic duty.

If there is one characteristic for a democratic system (besides the ballot itself) that is theoretically required, it is the capacity for and the practice of discussion. "It was true of the large as of the small society," says [A.D.] Lindsay, "that its health depends on the mutual understanding which discussion makes possible; and that discussion is the only possible instrument of its democratic government." How much participation in political discussion there is in the community, what it is, and among whom—these questions have been given answers . . . earlier. . . . In this instance there was little true discussion between the candidates, little in the newspaper commentary, little between the voters and the official party representatives, some within the electorate. On the grass roots level there was more talk than debate, and, at least inferentially, the talk had important effects upon voting, in reinforcing or activating the partisans if not in converting the opposition:

An assumption underlying the theory of democracy is that the citizenry has a strong motivation for participation in political life. But it is a curious quality of voting behavior that for large numbers of people motivation is weak if not almost absent. It is assumed that this motivation would gain its strength from the citizen's perception of the difference that alternative decisions made to him. Now when a person buys something or makes other decisions of daily life, there are direct and immediate consequences for him. But for the bulk of the American people the voting decision is not followed by any direct, immediate, visible personal consequences. Most voters, organized or unorganized, are not in a position to foresee the distant and indirect consequences for themselves, let alone the society. The ballot is cast, and for most people that is the end of it. If their side is defeated, "it doesn't really matter."

Knowledge

The democratic citizen is expected to be well informed about political affairs. He is supposed to know what the issues are, what their history is, what the relevant facts are, what alternatives are proposed, what the party stands for, what the likely consequences are. By such standards the voter falls short. Even when he has the motivation, he finds it difficult to make decisions on the basis of full information when the subject is relatively simple and proximate; how can he do so when it is complex and remote? The citizen is not highly informed on details of the campaign, nor does he avoid a certain misperception of the political situation when it is to his psychological advantage to do so. The electorate's perception of what goes on in the campaign is colored by emotional feeling toward one or the other issue, candidate, party, or social group.

Principle

The democratic citizen is supposed to cast his vote on the basis of principle—not fortuitously or frivolously or impulsively or habitually, but with reference to standards not only of his own interest but of the common good as well. Here, again, if this requirement is pushed at all strongly, it becomes an impossible demand on the democratic electorate.

Many voters vote not for principle in the usual sense but "for" a group to which they are attached—their group. The Catholic vote or the hereditary vote is explainable less as principle than as a traditional social allegiance. The ordinary voter, bewildered by the complexity of modern political problems, unable to determine clearly what the consequences are of alternative lines of action, remote from the arena, and incapable of bringing information to bear on principle, votes the way trusted people around him are voting. . . .

On the issues of the campaign there is a considerable amount of "don't know"—sometimes reflecting genuine indecision, more often meaning "don't care." Among those with opinions the partisans *agree* on most issues, criteria, expectations, and rules of the game. The supporters of the different sides disagree on only a few issues. Not, for that matter, do the candidates themselves always join the issue sharply and clearly. The partisans do not agree overwhelmingly with their own party's position, or, rather, only the small minority of highly partisan do; the rest take a rather moderate position on the political consideration involved in an election.

Rationality

The democratic citizen is expected to exercise rational judgment in coming to his voting decision. He is expected to have arrived at his principles by reason and to have considered rationally the implications and alleged consequences of the alternative proposals of the contending parties. Political theorists and commentators have always exclaimed over the seeming contrast here between requirement and fulfillment. . . . The upshot of this is that the usual analogy between the voting "decision" and the more or less carefully calculated decisions of consumers or businessmen or courts, incidentally, may be quite incorrect. For many voters political preferences may better be considered analogous to cultural tastes—in music, literature, recreational activities, dress, ethics, speech, social behavior. Consider the parallels between political preferences and general cultural tastes. Both have the origin in ethnic, sectional, class, and family traditions. Both exhibit stability and resistance to change for individuals but flexibility and adjustment over generations for the society as a whole. Both seem to be matters of sentiment and disposition rather than "reasoned preferences." While both are responsive to changed conditions and unusual stimuli, they are relatively invulnerable to direct argumentation and vulnerable to indirect social influences. Both are characterized more by faith than by conviction and by wishful expectation rather than careful prediction or consequences. The preference for one party rather than another must be highly similar to the preference for one kind of literature or music rather than another, and the choice of the same political party every four years may be parallel to the choice of the same old standards of conduct in new social situations. In short, it appears that a sense of fitness is a more striking feature of political preference than reason and calculation.

Requirements for the System

If the democratic system depended solely on the qualifications of the individual voter, then it seems remarkable that democracies have survived through the centuries. After examining the detailed data on how individuals misperceive political reality or respond to irrelevant social influences, one wonders how a democracy ever solves its political problems. But when one considers the data in a broader perpective—how huge segments of the society adapt to political conditions affecting them or how the political system adjusts itself to changing conditions over long periods of time—he cannot fail to be impressed with the total result. Where the rational citizen seems to abdicate, nevertheless angels seem to tread. . . .

That is the paradox. *Individual* voters today seem unable to satisfy the requirements for a democratic system of government outlined by political theorists. But the *system of democracy* does meet certain requirements for a going political organization. The individual members may not meet all the standards, but the whole nevertheless survives and grows. This suggests that where the classic theory is defective is in its concentration on the *individual* citizen. What are undervalued are certain collective properties that reside in the electorate as a whole and in the political and social system in which it functions.

The political philosophy we have inherited, then, has given more consideration to the virtues of the typical citizen of the democracy than to the working of the *system* as a whole. Moreover, when it dealt with the system, it mainly considered the single constitutive institutions of the system, not those general features necessary if the institutions are to work as required. For example, the rule of law, representative government, periodic elections, the party system, and the several freedoms of discussion, press, association, and assembly have all been examined by political philosophers seeking to clarify and to justify the idea of political democracy. But liberal democracy is more than a political system in which individual voters and political institutions operate. For political democracy to survive, other features are required: the intensity of conflict must be limited, the rate of change must be restrained, stability in the social and economic structure must be maintained, a pluralistic social organization must exist, and a basic consensus must bind together the contending parties.

Such features of the system of political democracy belong neither to the constitutive institutions nor to the individual voter. It might be said that they form the atmosphere or the environment in which both operate. In any case, such features have not been carefully considered by political philosophers, and it is on these broader properties of the democratic political system that more reflection and study by political theory is called for. In the most tentative fashion let us explore the values of the political system, as they involve the electorate, in the light of the foregoing considerations.

Underlying the paradox is an assumption that the population is homogeneous socially and should be homogeneous politically: that everybody is about the same in relevant social characteristics; that, if something is a political virtue (like interest in the election), then everyone should have it; that there is such a thing as "the" typical citizen on whom uniform requirements can be imposed. The tendency of classic democratic literature to work with an image of "the" voter was never justified. For, as we will attempt to illustrate

here, some of the most important requirements that democratic values impose on a system require a voting population that is not homogeneous but heterogeneous in its political qualities.

The need for heterogeneity arises from the contradictory functions we expect our voting system to serve. We expect the political system to adjust itself and our affairs to changing conditions; yet we demand too that it display a high degree of stability. We expect the contending interests and parties to pursue their ends vigorously and the voters to care; yet, after the election is over, we expect reconciliation. We expect the voting outcome to serve what is best for the community; yet we do not want disinterested voting unattached to the purposes and interests of different segments of that community. We want voters to express their own free and self-determined choices; yet, for the good of the community, we would like voters to avail themselves of the best information and guidance available from the groups and leaders around them. We expect a high degree of rationality to prevail in the decision; but were all irrationality and mythology absent, and all ends pursued by the most coldly rational selection of political means, it is doubtful if the system would hold together.

In short, our electoral system calls for apparently incompatible properties—which, although they cannot all reside in each individual voter, can (and do) reside in a heterogeneous electorate. What seems to be required of the electorate as a whole is a *distribution* of qualities along important dimensions. We need some people who are active in a certain respect, others in the middle, and still others passive. The contradictory things we want from the total require that the parts be different. This can be illustrated by taking up a number of important dimensions by which an electorate might be characterized.

Involvement and Indifference

How could a mass democracy work if all the people were deeply involved in politics? Lack of interest by some people is not without its benefits, too. True, the highly interested voters vote more, and know more about the campaign, and read and listen more, and participate more; however, they are also less open to persuasion and less likely to change. Extreme interest goes with extreme partisanship and might culminate in rigid fanaticism that could destroy democratic processes if generalized throughout the community. Low affect toward the election—not caring much—underlies the resolution of many political problems; votes can be resolved into a two-party split instead of fragmented into many parties (the splinter parties of the left, for example, splinter because their advocates are *too* interested in politics). Low interest provides maneuvering room for political shifts necessary for a complex society in a period of rapid change. Compromise might be based on sophisticated awareness of costs and returns—perhaps impossible to demand of a mass society—but it is more often induced by indifference. Some people are and should be highly interested in politics, but not everyone is or needs to be. Only the doctrinaire would deprecate the moderate indifference that facilitates compromise.

Hence, an important balance between action motivated by strong sentiments and action with little passion behind it is obtained by heterogeneity within the electorate. Balance of this sort is, in practice, met by a distribution of voters rather than by a homogeneous collection of "ideal" citizens.

Stability and Flexibility

Similar dimension along which an electorate might be characterized is stability-flexibility. The need for change and adaptation is clear, and the need for stability ought equally to be (especially from observation of current democratic practice in, say, certain Latin American countries). . . . [I]t may be that the very people who are most sensitive to changing social conditions are those most susceptible to political change. For, in either case, the people exposed to membership in overlapping strata, those whose former life-patterns are being broken up, those who are moving about socially or physically, those

who are forming new families and new friendships—it is they who are open to adjustments of attitudes and tastes. They may be the least partisan and the least interested voters, but they perform a valuable function for the entire system. Here again is an instance in which an individual "inadequacy" provides a positive service for society: The campaign can be a reaffirming force for the settled majority and a creative force for the unsettled minority. There is stability on both sides and flexibility in the middle.

Progress and Conservation

Closely related to the question of stability is the question of past versus future orientation of the system. In America a progressive outlook is highly valued, but, at the same time, so is a conservative one. Here a balance between the two is easily found in the party system and in the distribution of voters themselves from extreme conservatives to extreme liberals. But a balance between the two is also achieved by a distribution of political dispositions through time. There are periods of great political agitation (i.e., campaigns) alternating with periods of political dormancy. Paradoxically, the former—the campaign period—is likely to be an instrument of conservatism, often even of historical regression. . . .

Again, then, a balance (between preservation of the past and receptivity to the future) seems to be required of a democratic electorate. The heterogeneous electorate in itself provides a balance between liberalism and conservatism; and so does the sequence of political events from periods of drifting change to abrupt rallies back to the loyalties of earlier years.

Consensus and Cleavage. . .

[T]here are required *social* consensus and cleavage—in effect pluralism—in politics. Such pluralism makes for enough consensus to hold the system together and enough cleavage to make it move. Too much consensus would be deadening and restrictive of liberty; too much cleavage would be destructive of the society as a whole. . . . Thus again a requirement we might place on an electoral system—balance between total political war between segments of the society and total political indifference to group interests of that society—translates into varied requirements for different individuals. With respect to group or bloc voting, as with other aspects of political behavior, it is perhaps not unfortunate that "some do and some do not."

Individualism and Collectivism

Lord Bryce pointed out the difficulties in a theory of democracy that assumes that each citizen must himself be capable of voting intelligently:

> Orthodox democratic theory assumes that every citizen has, or ought to have, thought out for himself certain opinions, i.e., ought to have a definite view, defensible by argument, of what the country needs, of what principles ought to be applied in governing it, of the man to whose hands the government ought to be entrusted. There are persons who talk, though certainly very few who act, as if they believed this theory, which may be compared to the theory of some ultra-Protestants that every good Christian has or ought to have . . . worked out for himself from the Bible a system of theology.

In the first place, however, the information available to the individual voter is not limited to that directly possessed by him. True, the individual casts his own personal ballot. But, as we have tried to indicate . . . that is perhaps the most individualized action he takes in an election. His vote is formed in the midst of his fellows in a sort of group decision—if, indeed, it may be called a decision at all—and the total information and knowledge possessed in the group's present and past generations can be made available for the group's choice. Here is where opinion-leading relationships, for example, play an active role.

Second, and probably more important, the individual voter may not have a great deal of detailed information, but he usually has picked up the crucial *general* information as part of his social learning itself. He may not know the parties' position on the tariff, or who is for reciprocal trade treaties, or what are the differences on Asiatic policy, or how the parties split on civil rights, or how many security risks were exposed by whom. But he cannot live in an American community without knowing broadly where the parties stand. He has learned that the Republicans are more conservative and the Democrats more liberal—and he can locate his own sentiments and case his vote accordingly. After all, he must vote for one or the other party, and, if he knows the big thing about the parties, he does not need to know all the little things. The basic role a party plays as an institution in American life is more important to his voting than a particular stand on a particular issue.

It would be unthinkable to try to maintain our present economic style of life without a complex system of delegating to others what we are not competent to do ourselves, without accepting and giving training to each other about what each is expected to do, without accepting our dependence on others in many spheres and taking responsibility for their dependence on us in some spheres. And, like it or not, to maintain our present political style of life, we may have to accept much the same interdependence with others in collective behavior. We have learned slowly in economic life that it is useful not to have everyone a butcher or a baker, any more than it is useful to have no one skilled in such activities. The same kind of division of labor—as repugnant as it may be in some respects to our individualistic tradition—is serving us well today in mass politics. There is an implicit division of political labor within the electorate.

Chapter 14 Exercise

Explain how involvement in politics and indifference to political affairs are both necessary for our democratic system.

What is the major point of this essay? Identify the major theme and then utilize examples to bolster your perspective.

PART X

Strategy

CHAPTER 15

Scope of Conflict

The Contagiousness of Conflict

E. E. Schattschneider

Political scientist E. E. Schatttschneider introduces the scope of conflict in his classic book, The Semisovereign People. Schattschneider argues that politics is about conflict and the outcome of all conflict is determined by the scope of its contagion. As a consequence, the ". . . most important strategy of politics is concerned with the scope of conflict."

At the root of all politics is the universal language of conflict.

The central politic fact in a free society is the tremendous contagiousness of conflict.

Every fight consists of two parts: (1) the few individuals who are actively engaged at the center and (2) the audience that is irresistibly attracted to the scene. The spectators are as much a part of the over-all situation as are the overt combatants. The spectators are an integral part of the situation, for, as likely as not, the *audience* determines the outcome of the fight. The crowd is loaded with portentousness because it is apt to be a hundred times as large as the fighting minority, and the relations of the audience and the combatants are highly unstable. Like all other chain reactions, a fight is difficult to contain. To under-

stand any conflict it is necessary therefore to keep constantly in mind the relations between the combatants and the audience because the audience is likely to do the kinds of things that determine the outcome of the fight. This is true because the audience is overwhelming; it is never really neutral; the excitement of the conflict communicates itself to the crowd. *This is the basic pattern of all politics.*

The first proposition is that the outcome of every conflict is determined by the *extent* to which the audience becomes involved in it. That is, the outcome of all conflict is determined by the *scope* of its contagion. The number of people involved in any conflict determines what happens; every change in the number of participants, every increase or reduction in the number of participants, affects the result. Simply stated, the first proposition is that the intervention of Cole into a conflict between Able and Bart inevitably changes the nature of the conflict. Cole may join Able and tip the balance of forces in his favor, or he may support Bart and turn the balance the other way, or he may disrupt the conflict or attempt to impose his own resolution on both Able and Bart. No matter what he does, however, Cole will alter the conflict by transforming a one-to-one contest into a two-to-one conflict or a triangular conflict. Thereafter every new intervention, by Donald, Ellen, Frank, James, Emily, will alter the equation merely by enlarging the scope of conflict because each addition changes the balance of the forces involved. Conversely, every abandonment of the conflict by any of the participants changes the ratio.

The moral of this is: If a fight starts, watch the crowd, because the crowd plays the decisive role.

At the nub of politics are, first, the way in which the public participates in the spread of the conflict and, second, the processes by which the unstable relation of the public to the conflict is controlled.

The second proposition is a consequence of the first. The most important strategy of politics is concerned with the scope of conflict.

So great is the change in the nature of any conflict likely to be as a consequence of the widening involvement of people in it that the original participants are apt to lose control of the conflict altogether. Thus, Able and Bart may find, as the Harlem policeman and soldier found, that the fight they started has got out of hand and has been taken over by the audience. Therefore the contagiousness of conflict, the elasticity of its scope and the fluidity of the involvement of people are the X factors in politics.

Implicit in the foregoing propositions is another: It is extremely unlikely that both sides will be reinforced equally as the scope of the conflict is doubled or quadrupled or multiplied by a hundred or a thousand. That is, the balance of the forces recruited will almost certainly not remain constant. This is true because it is improbable that the participants in the original conflict con-

stitute a representative sample of the larger community; nor is it likely that the successive increments are representative. Imagine what might happen if there were a hundred times as many spectators on the fringes of the conflict who sympathized with Able rather than Bart. Able would have a strong motive for trying to spread the conflict while Bart would have an overwhelming interest in keeping it private. It follows that conflicts are frequently won or lost by the success that the contestants have in getting the audience involved in the fight or in excluding it, as the case may be.

Other propositions follow. It is one of the qualities of extremely small conflicts that the relative strengths of the contestants are likely to be known in advance. In this case the stronger side may impose its will on the weaker without an overt test of strength because people are apt not to fight if they are sure to lose. This is extremely important because the scope of conflict can be most easily restricted at the very beginning. On the other hand, the weaker side may have a great potential strength provided only that it can be aroused. The stronger contestant may hesitate to use his strength because he does not know whether or not he is going to be able to isolate his antagonist. Thus, the bystanders are a part of the calculus all conflicts And any attempt to forecast the outcome of a fight by estimating the strength of the original contestants is likely to be fatuous.

Every change in the scope of conflict has a bias; it is partisan in its nature. That is, it must be assumed that every change in the number of participants is about something, that the newcomers have sympathies or antipathies that make it possible to involve them. By definition, the intervening bystanders are not neutral. Thus, in political conflict every change in scope changes the equation.

Madison understood something about the relation of scope to the outcome of conflict. His famous essay No. 10 in the *Federalist Papers* should be reread in the context of this discussion.

> The smaller the society, the fewer probably will be the distinct parties and interests composing it, the more frequently will a majority be found of the same party; and the smaller

number of individuals composing a majority, and the smaller the compass within which they are placed, the more easily they will concert and execute their plans of oppression. Extend the sphere and you take in a greater variety of parties and interests; you make it less probable that a majority of the whole will have a common motive to invade the rights of other citizens.

The attempt to control the scope of conflict has a bearing on federal-state-local relations, for one way to restrict the scope of conflict is to *localize* it, while one way to expand it is to nationalize it. One of the most remarkable developments in recent American politics is the extent to which the federal, state, and local governments have become involved in *doing the same kinds of things* in large areas of public policy, so it is possible for contestants to move freely from one level of government to another in an attempt to find the level at which they might try most advantageously to get what they want. This development has opened up vast new areas for the politics of scope. It follows that debates about federalism, local self-government, centralization, and decentralization are actually controversies about the scale of conflict.

In the case of a village of 1,000 within a state having a population of 3,500,000, a controversy lifted from the local to the state or the national level multiplies its scope by 3,500 or 180,000 times. Inevitably the outcome of a contest is controlled by the level at which the decision is made. What happens when the scope of conflict is multiplied by 180,000? (1) There is a great probability that the original contestants will lose control of the matter. (2) A host of new considerations and complications are introduced, and a multitude of new resources for a resolution of conflict becomes available; solutions inconceivable at a lower level may be worked out at a higher level.

The nationalization of politics inevitably breaks up old local power monopolies and old sectional power complexes; as a matter of fact, the new dimension produces so great a change in the scale of organization and the locus of power that it may take on a semirevolutionary character. The

change of direction of party cleavages produced by the shift from sectional to national alignments has opened up a new political universe, a new order of possibilities and impossibilities.

The dynamics of the expansion of the scope of conflict are something like this:

1. Competitiveness is the mechanism for the expansion of the scope of conflict. It is the *loser* who calls in outside help. (Jefferson, defeated within the Washington administration, went to the country for support.) The expansion of the electorate resulted from party competition for votes. As soon as it becomes likely that a new social group will get the vote, *both* parties favor the extension. *This is the expanding universe of politics.* On the other hand, any attempt to monopolize politics is almost by definition an attempt to limit the scope of conflict.

2. Visibility is a factor in the expanding of the scope of conflict. A democratic government lives by publicity. This proposition can be tested by examining the control of publicity in undemocratic regimes.

3. The effectiveness of democratic government *as an instrument for the socialization of conflict depends on the amplitude of its powers and resources.* A powerful and resourceful government is able to respond to conflict situations by providing an arena for them, publicizing them, protecting the contestants against retaliation, and taking steps to rectify the situations complained of; it may create new agencies to hear new categories of complaints and take special action about them.

Every social institution is affected by the way in which its internal processes are publicized. For example, the survival of the family as a social institution depends to a great extent on its privacy. It is almost impossible to imagine what forces in society might be released if all conflict in the private domain were thrown open for public exploitation. Procedures for the control of the expansive power of conflict determine the shape of the political system.

There is nothing intrinsically good or bad about any given scope of conflict. Whether a large conflict is better than a small conflict depends on what the conflict is about and what people want to accomplish. A change of scope makes possible a new pattern of competition, a new balance of forces, and a new result, but it also *makes impossible a lot of other things.*

While the language of politics is often oblique and sometimes devious, it is not difficult to show that the opposing tendencies toward the privatization and socialization of conflict underlie all strategy.

The study of politics calls for a sense of proportion; in the present case it requires a sense of the relative proportions of the belligerents and the spectators. At the outset of every political conflict the relations of the belligerents and the audience are so unstable that it is impossible to calculate the strength of the antagonists because *all* quantities in the equation are indeterminate until all of the bystanders have been committed.

Political conflict is not like a football game, played on measured field by a fixed number of players in the presence of an audience scrupulously excluded from the playing field. Politics is much more like the original primitive game of football in which everybody was free to join, a game in which the whole population of one town might play the entire population of another town, moving freely back and forth across the countryside.

Many conflicts are narrowly confined by a variety of devices, but the distinctive quality of political conflicts is that the relations between the players and the audience have not been well defined and there is usually nothing to keep the audience from getting into the game.

Chapter 15 Exercise

Explain the scope of conflict and its importance for understanding politics. Be specific and utilize examples.

Why would losing parties wish to expand the scope of conflict?

CPSIA information can be obtained
at www.ICGtesting.com
Printed in the USA
LVOW02s0348101216
516656LV00007B/23/P